against the stream

against the stream

RALPH LEONARD

Peggy,

Thanks for your interest in the book and a special thanks for sharing your memories of Don.

Hope our paths cross again,

Ralph Leonard
2/19/09

CHAPEL HILL
PRESS, INC.

The poems of C. H. Lightbourn are included with the permission of his widow Bessie Lightbourn who resides in Nassau, Bahamas and I very much appreciate her act of kindness.

ISBN 1-59715-011-8
Library of Congress Catalog Number 2005932115

Printed in the United States of America
08 07 06 05 04   10 9 8 7 6 5 4 3 2 1

Published by Chapel Hill Press, Inc. | www.chapelhillpress.com

DEDICATION

This story is dedicated to my wife, Eileen who got me through some rough times and to my kids, Laurie, Ralph, and Scott who are always in my thoughts.

CONTENTS

ACKNOWLEDGMENTS

Many thanks are due the following people who were kind enough to give me their positive input and encouragement: Rachel Cashon, Kathy Chefas, Laurie Edgar (my daughter), Jeanne Fox, Larry Havill, Faye Thurston, and Ralph, Scott, Lisa and Leigh Leonard.

And to my ex-wife Gay who gave up most of her worldly possessions while we cruised in the Bahamas and beyond.

Also, a special thanks to Diana Spindler-Jones of the Chapel Hill Press for her efforts in improving the finished product.

⌣ CHAPTER ONE ⌣

"Eternal Father, Strong to save,
Whose arm hath bound the restless wave,
Who bid'st the mighty Ocean deep
Its own appointed limits keep;
O hear us when we cry to thee,
for those in peril on the sea."

THE NAVY HYMN

CROSSING THE GULF STREAM AT 3:00 A.M., Don did not need anything to divert his attention from the job at hand, which, this evening, was called survival. His primary concern was to try to find some pattern in the waves that seemed to be coming from every direction but the direction of the preceding wave. With a confused and primarily a following sea, this required him to constantly adjust the helm of his twenty-five-foot Robalo to ensure these waves did not become unwanted passengers. In addition, he was concerned that his cargo, although fairly well wrapped, did not suffer any more saltwater intrusion than necessary.

He did have one thing going for him. He had experience. His sensitivity to the not-so-subtle shifting of the sea beneath him sprang from years of exposure to small boats and the environment that they operated in.

Still, this did not keep him from questioning his reason for being out on this moonless cruise. The fact that the moon was missing was, after all, by design. The darker it was, the better it was.

1

What had happened to the idealist who had lived for years outside the socioeconomic system that most of society seemed to be immersed in?

Was this really worth the improvement of his economic lot in life?

At what point did the barter system fail to meet most of the requirements for maintaining his rather individualized lifestyle?

Why had fate dictated this method, for a gifted son of working class parents, to rise a few rungs on that illusional ladder called success?

He was contemplating all of this while still trying to control his boat. The surge of the sea was a pressing backdrop to the battle for the control of his consciousness. It was the need to focus on his seamanship versus the ill-timed flood of retrospection that were both competing for his attention.

Could he afford to lapse into a state of reflection or was the choice his to make?

Apparently, it was not, since thoughts of his early childhood began to flood his mind.

The year was 1943 and although Don could not remember his birth that year or even much else from those first five years, he did have his memory of pictures from that period to help fill in the blanks.

The place was Vallejo, California. His dad, a sergeant in the army, was there doing his part for the war effort, protecting the naval shipyard at Mare Island from an air attack. His father's responsibilities had included manning several anti-aircraft gun emplacements located in the sand traps of the Pebble Beach Golf Course, some miles to the south. Tough duty, but someone had to do it. His dad had been in the service when the war broke out and he had continued to serve his country for a total of twenty-seven years.

Had his dad, who had been given a lot of natural talent, squandered his abilities by serving his country for so many years or had he been using the service as a means to escape the burden that God-given abilities can place upon a person?

Was his dad patriotic or had those childhood marches of himself and his brother around the breakfast table to John Phillips Sousa just been contrived to keep them out of trouble?

2

Robalo on Calmer Day

It seemed important on this particular moonless night to reach some definitive conclusion on this matter. As a youngster, Don had been proud of his father and the uniform that he had worn. It was only as he had grown older that his father's image began to take a beating. However, pictures and the recall of his dad's reminiscences, as Don was growing up, allowed him to imagine his childhood at this time.

Don's ears were ever attentive to the drone of his two, 150-HP Mercury engines, which he hoped would not cause him any consternation on this trip. This boat was much bigger and more heavily powered than his old fifteen-foot single-engine 65-HP riverboat. His old boat had ferried him safely across this Gulf Stream many times. He was still breaking-in the Robalo, and he never felt comfortable with the security that two engines supposedly offered. In his mind, the potential for twice the number of problems, from these more complex and more difficult to work on engines, offset any theoretical advantage that they offered. He was of the old school. His feeling was that if you only had one engine you were more apt to make sure that it was running properly. Also, he was an ardent advocate of keeping things simple. Time spent in the Bahamas had made him quite aware of the consequences that mechanical failure there presented. Reliable mechanical help was scarce, and the process of obtaining replacement parts was sure to add days to the task of repairing any type of breakdown. The magnification of the dollars spent remedying a breakdown was also a big factor, and dollars were one thing that Don did not usually possess in any abundance.

After the war, Don's father moved the family back to Maine, which was where his dad had been born and raised. The contrast between the San Francisco Bay area of California and rural Maine was glaring enough that even a boy, barely three years old, was impacted by the change.

Memories of his Grandparent's cottage at Schoodic Lake and kerosene lanterns, wood burning stoves, water supplied from hand-operated well pumps, outhouses, crank type telephones, and dirt roads had become permanently ensconced in Don's mind. Over the course of subsequent years, Don was able to observe his grandparents become beneficiaries of more modern ways to cope with daily existence. In their rural cottage, leased from a timber company for about eighty dollars a year, which represented property taxes, his grandparents never did have running water or inside plumbing.

Shit!! Don struggled to keep his balance as a particularly aggressive wave struck the starboard quarter of his boat. Don felt that he should soon be seeing the lights that perched atop some of the higher condos that dotted the coast of south Florida. He hated these condos as much as anyone who had grown up in this part of Florida before they had sprouted from the sand. "The Great Wall of Atlantis" was how he referred to this aberration. After all, it did shield the ever-billowing population of coastal Florida from any invasion by the survivors of the lost civilization of Atlantis. Wasn't it rumored that this continent had sunk not far off the coast? It also served as an effective means of keeping the people who could not afford oceanfront property from gaining access to the beaches, and that really pissed off Don.

On a night like this, though, he was able to suppress his hostility toward the denizens of these condos. The high-rises did serve as an excellent aid to navigation. Their lights were perched far higher than anything the Coast

4

Guard provided in the way of buoys, channel markers, or even lighthouses. Picking up these lights on the horizon was always comforting. With fifteen miles still to go, it provided a means of orientation. Having been pushed around by the wind, the waves, and the Gulf Stream for the past five hours, Don was anxious to know his exact position.

While living in Portland, Maine, Don could still vaguely remember his brother reading to him. Since they were kids, his brother had provided a sounding board as well as a basis for comparison to many of his later actions—he was the yin to his yang. Later, the military moved the family to El Paso, but there was no interruption in the stories that his brother had shared with him. In fact, this process evolved into Don's learning to read long before his teachers entered the picture. This early interest in reading evolved into a lifelong love of books. He enjoyed the varying viewpoints and ideas that books introduced. Reading accelerated the exposure rate to new facts and ideas. It was faster than waiting for a life experience to deliver this information.

Wham!! Now the boat lurched forward as a wave from almost directly astern pushed it down into a trough at a faster rate than the engine speed alone would have dictated. Don nudged the throttles in order to catch up with the back of the wave that was trying to leave him wallowing in a chasm. He was now back in sync with the flow of the sea.

Memories of foxholes dug in the desert sands of El Paso and tumbleweed piled high came into his head. He was hiding from his brother who, armed with a shiny new cap gun, was searching for him.

There had also been an effort to emulate Superman. With a scarf tied to his back, he had jumped from a second-floor wooden fire escape of a converted barracks, which served as base housing. His attempt ended abruptly when he found out that he was not aerodynamically designed for that purpose. A broken arm and a new respect for Superman were the result of this life experience. Too bad he had not encountered this in his reading yet.

He also vividly remembered countless trips to the NCO (Non Commissioned Officers) club with his parents. The men who had flown

5

in the bombers during World War II had many great stories to tell. The service was still comprised of many veterans, who really enjoyed their jobs. His dad had transferred to the air force when it became a separate branch of the service after the war.

Salt spray, which was a constant irritant on most of his trips across the Stream, was beginning to take its toll. The cumulative effect of the exposure caused his eyes to sting, despite the use of a diving mask to protect them from this nemesis. The mask would have to be frequently cleaned. His eyes were most vulnerable to the airborne particles of sodium while he attended to this task.

The spray left him chilled. Again, he had memories of sitting shivering next to his brother on the edge of that Olympic size pool on the base in El Paso, the place that he had learned to swim. He only had five years under his cowboy belt at the time, but he already sensed the thrill and pleasure that being immersed in water brought him, excluding bathwater of course.

As his third grade year of school began, Don could remember the house on Smith Street back in Bangor, Maine. It seemed to be a big house at the time; however, Don was all too well aware of how reality had a way of shrinking the size of past memories, especially those of youth. He had broken his arm again, when his toboggan failed to negotiate a bend on downward sloping Smith Street. At least none of his memories of those eighteen months contained any of the monsters similar to those Stephen King had imagined while a resident of that small city with its interesting past.

As the boat continued to bob and yaw under the ceaseless procession of waves, he fought to forestall the onset of seasickness which was always trying to invade his body, even though he had spent countless hours on the water over the years.

Thoughts of Denver and his fourth grade year were a welcome means of keeping his mal de mer at bay. The house with the picture window that afforded a view of the mountains was actually in Aurora, which was a fairly new suburb at the time.

His parents had made two purchases while living there that would

6

more or less affect his later life. They had bought a piano and a television. Well, they had been right about the television, but the piano was a waste.

His mother's job as a nurse led her to work weekends. It was not unusual for his dad, while babysitting, to take both Don and Ralph to the horse track and the dog track. This was apparently legal at the time. Don wondered if his lifelong disdain for gambling had been born there or if it was the result of subsequent gambling forays by his father. His dad did not curtail his lifestyle to accommodate his boys, but rather took them along wherever he went. Dad's other weekend haunts were one of the local taverns or the NCO club on the base.

Don glanced at his watch to see how he was doing compared with his schedule. He needed to be through the inlet by 4:30 A.M. This would give him some leeway. His efforts were aimed at avoiding any law enforcement officials who might be disguised as pleasure boaters or fishermen. They would use the rock breakers at the inlet as a perch for observing incoming boat traffic. He had chosen Monday night to come across. The Marine Patrol and the Sheriff's Patrol usually had Monday evening off. This was their reward for spending a busy weekend ensuring that the large area's boating population was complying with the law. His biggest concern was the Coast Guard, which maintained a base just inside the Palm Beach inlet. Their movements were more random in nature and his boat would have aroused instant suspicion at that hour.

His mind continued to wander, almost chronologically, through those earlier years. After Denver, there was that summer in Biloxi, Mississippi when the family's meager financial resources had seemed to be stretched to their limit. For a couple of days their meals had consisted of just bread and cinnamon. Then he and his brother had found an old crab net. They were able to beg a few scraps of meat from a kindly butcher. Using the meat as bait, they somehow managed to catch about a dozen crabs. This feat was accomplished at the local pier. It was only a block or so to the little house that the family was renting. They soon presented this gift of food to their mom. She seemed appreciative until the crabs leaped from the boiling

7

pot when she tried to immerse them. The crabs started scurrying about her kitchen floor. Dad rushed to the rescue with a lid for the pot and with quick reflexes recaptured the wandering crustaceans.

From Biloxi, the family relocated to Metairie, a suburb of New Orleans. His fifth year of school was a faded memory. What had not faded was the combination bus and streetcar trips downtown. Canal Street would always evoke visions filled with an almost overwhelming bombardment of things new and different. His psyche was still young and impressionable. His parents had taken him to Mardi Gras. There were the trips that he and Ralph took by themselves. Following an afternoon movie, they would just wander around the town, soaking in the sights and absorbing the energy that the metropolis radiated. This did not seem a neglectful act on the part of his parents; instead, it seemed a trusting act and a vote of confidence in the ability of the two boys to conduct themselves prudently.

This trust or confidence was further evidenced at the beginning of that summer when he and Ralph boarded a train bound for their grandparents' cottage in Maine. Of course, Travelers Aid in New York City met them and the conductor had been personally asked to keep his eye on them. Adelaide and Bunny, their aunt and uncle, had met them at South Station in Boston. Naturally, while there, Uncle Bunny, a truck driver and World War II vet, had to make the rounds of the local Irish taverns to show off his two nephews. Following a brief stay, they boarded the Maine Central Railroad at North Station. An old steam driven engine would take them the final miles to Milo, Maine.

APPROACHING THE INLET, Don turned back the boat into the waves that had been chasing him for the past few hours while he surveyed the entrance as best he could. It was already apparent that his timing in relation to the tide was not good. The tidal current was flowing rapidly out of the inlet. The waves, which were being driven by the strong onshore wind, were building up at the mouth of this break in the shoreline that allowed boats access to the much calmer Lake Worth and the Intracoastal Waterway.

Funny that one of his first memories of West Palm Beach, which was where the family had relocated after leaving New Orleans in 1954, was of this same inlet. Shortly after their arrival, his dad had bought masks and flippers for both him and his brother. The place that they had tested these new gifts was this very inlet. That initial diving experience had been spectacular. Don knew right away that the world that existed just below the surface offered an escape from its counterpart, which lurked only a few feet above. The possibility of escape did not take on that much importance until later years. At that moment, it was the beauty aspect that enthralled him the most.

His flashback to that first time at the inlet was not a strange occurrence for him. Almost every time he came through it, he thought back to that first visit to its rocky breakers.

He circled the boat a couple of times to satisfy himself that the coast was clear. The throttles were constantly adjusted to avoid broaching the boat as he entered this churning passage. A path to calmer waters, the inlet had been his target for the past few hours. A minor increase in his heart rate marked the accomplishment of his objective. He took great pride in his boat handling abilities. Don knew there were only a few captains who would attempt this inlet under these conditions. A list of those captains would shrink even more when confronted with doing so at night.

Continuing through the inlet, he turned his boat north, opting to pass close to the Sailfish Marina docks. He chose this route rather than going straight to the Port of Palm Beach and then west of Peanut Island. That course would have taken him right by the Coast Guard base. Winding to the left, he continued to follow the shore until he could turn right and pass underneath the Blue Heron Bridge. Anyone awake at this hour would have noted his outriggers and probably just thought, "There goes another foolish fisherman." Of course, he was heading in at a time when most really dedicated anglers would be heading out.

With a couple of miles to go before reaching his destination, he allowed a sense of elation to sweep through his being. This sweep was in an almost inverse relation to the ebb of adrenaline departing from his system. Don had come out on top, at least this round, in the battle with his constant adversary, the sea. Although he had viewed the ocean as an opponent for this evening, he normally viewed it as a friend. This was just another competition between soul mates. God knows that if Don was anything, he was competitive.

Once he had exited Lake Worth with a turn to port, he idled his boat under normally busy U.S. Highway 1. Proceeding west, he made yet another turn into a canal that led into the village of North Palm Beach.

There were no stevedores waiting to unload his cargo. This was not a union operation, unless you considered the loosely associated Good Old Boy Network as a part of organized labor. Soon he was secured to a dock behind a medium-size house in a slightly upscale neighborhood. The three guys who then quickly unloaded his cargo did so in a quiet and rapidly efficient manner in what remained of the darkness. Only the paperboy was stirring at this hour, and his deliveries were to the front of the house and not to the back.

AS THE SUN MADE ITS APPEARANCE, Don was underway again, disguised as just another fisherman out to test his luck and his skills. This was the late '70s and Don didn't involve himself with the moral issues of marijuana. He didn't deal drugs. His specialty was simply transporting them as a means to make a living. Don was able to put the skills that he possessed to good use as a means for improving his economic status, and isn't that what most people try to do? So what if he didn't have to punch in, and so what if he was working in an environment that he loved. He was truly an independent contractor.

Don decided to grace his mother with his presence, since he needed to wait two days before collecting the money due to him for his previous night's work. Her house in North Palm Beach was not on the water. Her carport provided a good place for storing his old Bronco, which had been customized to exclude its top. It was his nondescript form of land transportation that offered maximum exposure to the sun. Despite his

10

Irish/English, genetically sensitized skin, he led a life of constant exposure to the yellow orb that dominated the sky over his domain, which included the Bahamas as well as south Florida.

His mother's yard also provided a safe and convenient place to bury his coffee cans that were full of cash. Coffee cans were preferred over the more conventional safety deposit boxes offered by the banks. He had always been on a cash basis, having never opened a checking account, and only once for a short time did he possess a credit card.

His mother would enjoy the company as long as he kept his drinking under control. However, despite his love for her and his appreciation for all of her sacrifices, too much alcohol seemed to unleash an abusive side of Don that was very difficult for him to control. This abusiveness manifested itself, no matter whom he was with, whenever he passed a certain threshold in his drinking. The threshold was a moving target depending on who he was with and the mood that he had been in when the drinking for that day had started. It was also impacted by the food that he had consumed.

He didn't directly blame his mother for the death of his dad in 1970. But his basic intolerance for ineptness in general often made him wonder what would have happened if things had turned out differently on the beach, that day of his father's heart attack. Only a week before his death, the doctors at the VA hospital had wanted to admit him after detecting problems with his heart. His dad had developed general contempt for doctors. They had recently botched an operation to improve the circulation in his left leg. He had said, "Those doctors are not going to make a cardiac invalid out of me." At that time, heart bypass operations were very risky. The operations were by no means routine.

The day of his dad's demise, he and Don's mother were spending a relaxing day on Juno Beach. This was a somewhat isolated community back in 1970. Dad had gone swimming well offshore. This was something that he never did. A former Eagle Scout and an excellent swimmer in his youth, Dad felt the beach was a place to drink beer and look at the pretty girls. While walking out of the water, he was stricken with a heart attack, and despite all of her nurse's training, Don's mother froze and did not respond to the situation. By the time the ambulance got to Juno Beach, it was too late for his father.

TWO DAYS AFTER DELIVERING HIS CARGO, Donnie, as he was better known in the islands, was on his way back to Treasure Cay in the Abacos. Now the weather was nicer, and he had his Robalo up on a plane. It would be a much shorter trip, except that he planned to clear immigration at West End where he knew most of the locals. Again, his thoughts drifted to a simpler time, even though most people thought that his lifestyle, now, was far from complex.

When his family arrived in West Palm, Don had been hesitant to get close to any of his newfound friends, and there were many. He was popular with his classmates. Finally, after two years in the same house, he had sensed a change in his dad's attitude about moving. The family had rented a small old stucco house that lacked both air conditioning (usual at that time) and a good exposure to the prevailing winds. Nonetheless, it was fine with both of the boys and their mother. She had found a good job as a nurse at St. Mary's Hospital.

Two years after his transfer to the air base in West Palm, his dad made the decision to leave the family there while he spent the next eighteen months in Alaska. When this happened, Don's whole attitude toward friendships began to change. He also sensed a change in the relationship with his brother, who had always been his best friend during those years they had bounced from place to place. Although only one year apart in school, they had a different circle of friends, and they spent less time with each other. Still, his brother was his main confidant. He also competed with his brother. Didn't all brothers compete in some way or another?

He thought of always being short for his age, but he never let this hold him back, and in the long run, it was probably an asset, at least to the extent that it spurred him to achieve. His grades were excellent, and he participated in sports as well as became a class officer. His time spent working at Anthony's Ranch, west of town, held special meaning for him. There were also the camping trips and the rum soaked cigars that he and his buddies smoked while drinking a couple of cans of beer.

Don couldn't quite remember what precipitated his running away the summer between his junior and senior years, but he was sure there was a principle involved. He had been angry when his grandmother called his parents to tell them that he was in Lake View. It had been a long bus trip to Maine and he had hitchhiked for the last part of the way. Certainly, this had nothing to do with his brother leaving for the navy, but he had missed him.

His recollection had him returning to West Palm for the start of his senior year. Mother had wired the money for the ticket home. Maine hadn't been the same as it was the last summer that he and Ralph had spent there, three years earlier. They had explored old logging roads, picked beans and blueberries, fished, and played baseball. They had also tested their grandparents' patience with some of their antics, which included catching rides aboard the old steam engines and cabooses of the Canadian Pacific Railroad. No tickets were required for these rides. It was not as if they were hobos. When the trains would pull onto the siding there in Lake View, the boys would plead with the engineer or brakeman for a chance to hop on. The old engineers weren't encumbered with worries of insurance companies, which would certainly prohibit that practice now.

Don on right with his brother at his grandparents' house on Schoodic Lake.

Getting lost while exploring in the woods had not helped Grandma's nerves any either. Following old logging roads, they would occasionally stumble upon an abandoned logging shack. Treasures often existed in these crumbling remnants that had been built to house the isolated men who had worked the forests. There were

13

treasures in the form of old magazines. Hunters had long since removed any things of value, but the old magazines often remained. *Stag* was one that Don could still recall. Drawings of early pinup girls evoked fond memories. While he and Ralph would be catching up on their reading, Grandma would be fretting not knowing whether to send out search parties.

AS HE APPROACHED WEST END, his thoughts faded while he looked for the markers. The markers leading the way into Bahamian harbors were usually obscure. There was no reason to get lost here. He had entered this harbor countless times. After checking in with the uniformed officials and after topping off his tanks, time was spent catching up on the local gossip before slipping out of the harbor. Soon his boat was passing Memory Rock and heading across the banks for Treasure Cay.

Not one to normally reminisce, Don wondered if this last, tough trip triggered a past life review in the hopes of bringing some sense to his life's journey to date? It was certainly a road less traveled. Was this an attempt to find out at what point he had reached the fork in his road? Nothing here in his memories seemed to have any dark stigma attached to it. He groped for some chink in the armor that might have allowed the penetration of some life-altering occurrence. These were memories that he was sure millions of boys had shared and there was nothing to cull him from the herd of his peers. Of course, he was right at the cusp of the generation of baby boomers. As a senior member of this fraternity, he had been exposed to all of the things that supposedly shaped his generation.

⌒ CHAPTER TWO ⌒

"The mass of men lead lives of quiet desperation."

THOREAU

AFTER SETTLING IN ON HIS FORTY-FOOT HOUSEBOAT, the *Oar Dog*, and with money in his pocket, it was time to party. Just sitting on a lawn chair in his Speedo (Speedos made up 90% of his wardrobe when he was wearing any clothes at all) and his straw hat with his vodka and orange juice, he was able to attract a party. Tourists and locals alike tended to congregate when Donnie was holding court. The visitors could sense and the locals knew that what might start as idle chatter would evolve into an afternoon of diving and volleyball and probably just balling in general. He was the catalyst for a break in anyone's daily humdrum existence. If you chose to go boating or diving with Donnie, you had to comply with the rules of the captain of the boat, and one rule stated that all female crew members remove their tops once out of the marina or sooner if they wished. Donnie, himself, boated without any suit at all, and he encouraged this from his passengers, although it was optional. Most people seemed to take advantage of this opportunity to liberate their bodies from the confinement of their suits, but in truth, they were really liberating their libidos from the confinement of society in general.

It took a strong constitution to remain functioning at the end of a day of revelry with Donnie. Physical exertion, exposure to the sun, and the consumption of alcohol, grass, and cocaine took its toll on even the hardiest of souls.

15

As Don sat in his favorite chair sipping on his first drink of the day, he began his morning ritual of removing the cobwebs from his brain. This usually consisted of reviewing the previous day's events in order to determine if there was anyone or anything that he might want to include in today's activities. Was there any new acquaintance whose company he enjoyed enough to share parts of today's agenda with? Had he made any commitments while under the influence that needed to be modified this morning? While most people were worried about getting to work on time, fighting with traffic or their spouses, dealing with their bosses or their customers, Donnie's primary concerns were how much fun was he going to have, and who would be involved? As strange as it may seem, this could be stressful in its own way, but he didn't expect to get much sympathy.

By the time he started his second drink, he usually had things pretty well sorted out. He would then, typically, grab the current book that he was reading and immerse himself in it until the less hardy began to stir. It was often late in the morning before the previous day's revelers were ready to start another round. The attrition rate for this group was high. Many were vacationers who were trying to compress their life into a one or two week vacation. They just weren't conditioned to handle what was an ongoing lifestyle for Don, who had been at this for more than ten years.

Palm Beach High Days.

HE PUT HIS BOOK DOWN FOR A MINUTE AND THOUGHT TO HIMSELF, had it been ten years since he had come to the Islands?

What had transpired during that nine-year period beginning with his senior year of high school and ending when he left for the islands with his standard size Igloo, which was crammed with clothes and diving gear?

16

He recalled the devastation he felt the day his friend Butch had been killed. The car that he and Butch had spent so much time in together was pulverized by a Florida East Coast freight train just a few blocks away from where Butch had just dropped off Don. Don had grappled with all of the whys and the what ifs.

He also recalled missing his brother's presence. That had surprised Don, since there had always been that pressure to compete with Ralph. His recollection was murky as to what had driven him to join the navy. Did this have anything to do with his brother? The odds were against them ever seeing much of each other, especially since Ralph was on a ship in Japan at the time. But the odds were wrong, weren't they? What twist of fate led them both to end up at submarine school in New London within a week of each other?

While waiting for their class to start, they had great times on liberty together in New York City and Boston. They hit the Big Apple completely underdressed for the nightlife. Both brothers had purchased cheap sport coats so that they could get into the Peppermint Twist Lounge. Bribing the doorman, they gained entrance to this popular nightspot and the privilege to pay exorbitant prices for drinks. The small town Lotharios turned on their charm and they met a couple of hot female prospects. Could he and his brother see them home? the girls had asked. So two guys, who had no idea of where they were going, escorted the girls on the subway. At 4:00 A.M., Don and Ralph found out that the girls just needed protection, not the passion the guys had in mind. With a little luck, the brothers found their way back downtown and subsequently back to New London. Oh well!

They were a little luckier on their trip to Boston. The guys had met two chicks at Revere Beach. Don and his brother were in their element on the beach. The girls were impressed, and a good time was had by all.

Returning to New London, their reunion was cut short. Their time together had been interrupted when Don was accepted at the U.S. Naval Academy at Annapolis.

Lost in reverie, Donnie was oblivious to the two bikini clad, slightly chunky but pretty Swiss girls walking down the dock toward the *Oar Dog*.

17

On Leave from the Naval Academy

Whenever his thoughts regressed to his days at Annapolis, Don's heart rate would increase. Nothing in his memory stirred up the kind of reaction that seized him when he thought of his two-and-a-half years stay there.

The "Marble Monastery" was how he referred to his home for that period. He had taken a vow, but he had been so naive. The overall experience had left a dark imprint on him; however, it had not always been that way. It had been bright at the beginning, those early days at the academy.

He readily embraced the competitive spirit that abounded at the academy. Don was not physically big, but each of the 150 pounds that comprised his body was packed with excess energy and driven by a strong desire to compete. Pushups, chin-ups, sit-ups, whatever the navy required, Don easily exceeded.

Don got along well with his shipmates. He wore his uniform with pride.

There was an unusual concentration of cadets from Palm Beach High School. Two friends had been two years ahead of Don in high school, and four had been in the class ahead of him. Because of the one-year delay in Don's gaining entrance, these friends were now upperclassmen. It didn't hurt to have friends in high places.

Annapolis was steeped in tradition, and Don was sensitive to this as he trained. The army versus navy football game was a tradition that particularly appealed to him. During the summer of his second year, he had met a girl from Pittsburgh. She was attending college there. He wanted to invite Jeanie to the big game in Philadelphia. Actually, he wanted to party with her after the game. The midshipmen sat together during the game, so this precluded any fraternizing with the fairer sex.

The problem was getting her to Philadelphia. She had no money and neither did he. A phone call to his brother, now serving on a submarine home, ported in Norfolk, solved the problem. In return for a ticket to the game and a date with one of Joanie's cute friends, Ralph agreed to drive to

18

Pittsburgh, pick up the girls, and then drive to Philadelphia for the game. After the game and the parties, his brother would reverse the trip of about 750 miles each way. What are brothers for? Ralph had loaned Don his car that previous summer for a trip back to West Palm, and Don knew the girls would be impressed with the three-year-old Ford convertible.

Don hated to say goodbye to Joanie after the round of parties, but the midshipmen had to board busses en-masse for the trip back to Maryland. Joanie did write later to tell him that it was a little chilly in November to be in a convertible with no heater. Didn't she know that Florida cars at that time sometimes came without heaters in order to hold the price down.

His record and his grades were good until the fall term of his third year. The incident that finally triggered his rebellion was his being written up while he was on hall watch when he had left his post for a minute to use the bathroom.

Well, piss on them if they wanted to be so petty. He had seen too many good guys lose their identity in an effort to play the game in the manner dictated by this prestigious institution. Don did not like how the institution had changed his friends during their time at the academy. It had become intolerable to watch many shipmates, whom he liked, change over during this period of time. Also, his failing eyesight would have kept him out of flight school, which was a major letdown.

When he confronted his superiors with his request to leave the "Monastery," they were shocked. Why would an individual, who had already endured most of the hazing and weeding out process, want to give up a chance to be an officer in the U.S. Navy? After he had told the Navy that they could shove it, they asked him to see the chaplain. He confided to the chaplain:, "I don't think if there was really a god that he would have intended for me to hone my skills at warfare here at the Marble Monastery." He went on to tell him that he thought that God would be more peaceably inclined. Don recalled that his early readings of Emerson and Thoreau did not mesh too well with his life at the academy. Donald did not share the opinion of his superiors as to what he was giving up. In

19

his mind, he wasn't throwing anything away; but, in fact, he was regaining the opportunity to reestablish his own identity. He remembered how his mother had felt that a change occurred in him when he was knocked out while boxing at the academy. Yes, it was true that he had been unconscious, all right, but this had been the result of his submission to the system those first two years, not the boxing.

In an unusual twist of fate, Don was forced to hit a person in order to get out of jail. Normally, it was the other way around. Carefully weighing his alternatives, Don decided on an extreme means of getting the attention of his advisors. Striking a senior officer was the course that he chose. Don apologized to his senior officer before striking him. The blow was more symbolic than damaging. This was the only recourse the navy had given him. Maybe they would understand now that he was serious. He was honorably discharged shortly thereafter.

AFTER LEAVING ANNAPOLIS, Don spent several months bumming around. He renewed old acquaintances and spent time diving off the reefs that

Speared On Reef Off of Palm Beach

stretched along the coast of south Florida. On a typical day, he would drive to the beach, park his car, and swim out to the reefs.

Seeking employment, he found it west of town. A plant that provided liquid gasses to Pratt & Whitney hired him. Working the night shift, he was able to go diving during the day.

This was nice for a while; however, he felt something was lacking. With two and a half years of college credits and his military obligation behind him, he enrolled at the University of Florida with hopes of fulfilling his ambition, at the time, of becoming a

20

veterinarian. This ambition had lain pretty well dormant since his high school days when he had worked at Anthony's Ranch.

Three things conspired to keep him from achieving this goal: the realization of how long it would take, the money that would be required, and the most dramatic reason, Rachel.

The two girls had paused near the *Oar Dog*, hoping to catch Don's eye. Actually, even as he had been regressing at a subconscious level, he had been checking them out on a less cerebral plane. Two possible new crewmates? He wouldn't mind further checking out what little their suits left to reveal.

However, they would have to wait until he got through with his reflections, because his feelings were stirring up remembrances from a period that certainly had altered the course of his life.

When he met Rachel, she seemed to satisfy his criteria for a woman with whom he would like to spend more time. She had recently graduated and was living in Jacksonville where she had taken a teaching job. She was in good shape; she liked the outdoors; she had a good sense of humor; and she was pretty. They had enjoyed each other's company as he struggled to balance the party atmosphere against the academic demands of Gainesville. This balancing act was especially difficult for Don who was coming from the rigid, monk-like environment that existed at the academy. Female classmates were a novelty that caused his eyes and then his mind to wander from the studies at hand.

The shock was overwhelming when at the end of his first term Rachel informed him that she was pregnant. Their first sexual encounter had led to this situation. He had been worried about grades, and now he was confronted with a life-altering event. Both his and Rachel's lives were suddenly in disarray. They cared for each other, but they really didn't know each other.

There was an initial sense of responsibility for his part in creating the situation that he was in, but he also held Rachel accountable. How could she have let this happen? Fair or not, he felt betrayed.

They decided that marriage should be the first step. This was accomplished on their second attempt at elopement. The first ended when Rachel stated

21

that she wanted marriage to be more than just a ceremony for giving their child a name. Still, he felt that his child should bear his name. So after discussions with the potential grandparents and other confidants, they made a second trip over the border to Georgia, where they were married.

A decision was made to move to California, thereby minimizing the interfacing they would have to do with family and friends. They did not feel the need for any elaborate support systems, although the term *support system* wasn't really in vogue at that time.

Don had no trouble finding a job with a company once they had relocated to California. They settled in to await the birth of their child. California, the state that has been a magnet for so many, held little appeal for him. His circumstances isolated him from the water, and when he did gain access to it, he found it too cold for his liking. This put him in the position of biding his time, and patience was one thing that he did not possess in any quantity.

Then there was Dave and his wife, who were neighbors. Dave had gotten behind with his rent, which required him to come up with money that he didn't have. From the beginning, Don's intuition had told him that this guy couldn't be trusted. When he approached Don and Rachel for a loan, Don let his instinct to help people overrule his gut intuition about the guy. They loaned him money from their savings. These savings were being set aside for expenses relating to the impending birth of their baby. Don recalled emphasizing to Dave how important it was that this loan be repaid in a timely manner. Dave assured them that this would be the case.

Don was making a decent salary, and Rachel was working, so it didn't take them long to join the mainstream of consumer driven Americans. He purchased a green MG convertible with the help of the Bank of America. This was his first and only new car.

When Leigh was born in July, Don was proud to be the father of a healthy new baby. During this era, even caring fathers were not as involved in the birthing process as they are today. Don did not get too involved in the changing of diapers, or the feeding, but on one occasion, he bundled

Leigh up and loaded her into his little convertible for a trip to the clinic. He recalled being the only father there and wondered how he had managed to cope with the delays that they had encountered. However, it soon became apparent that he was not ready to fulfill the role of a parent. He truly felt like a fish out of the water. His relationship with Rachel had deteriorated when she had discovered that he was having an affair with a fellow worker. His behavior and his actions were clearly an indication of how ill suited he was in the role of a family man. He hated California and his eight-to-five job. There was also a grudge to settle with Dave, who had left the state without repaying his loan and who was now residing in Oklahoma.

Don knew in his heart that his daughter would probably suffer the most from having the misfortune of being conceived by a father who just didn't quite fit into the mold. This bothered him and he had regrets, but there was a force from within urging him to get underway.

HIS FIRST STOP WAS OKLAHOMA. When he knocked on Dave's door, the deadbeat was fortunate that he did not open it wide. Dave had barely cracked the door open when he realized who was visiting. Don confronted Dave with the fact that he had promised to pay back the money, which he knew had been earmarked for their baby, in a timely manner. When Dave defaulted, Don instantly considered him to be lower than a low life. Dave slammed the door shut in Don's face. Don responded by going back to his car and retrieving his pistol. He then calmly walked back and emptied its cylinder into the door, while shouting at Dave that he would be back if Rachel didn't promptly receive the money owed. Dave called the police, but Don had already jumped into his MG and headed east.

The month was January and it had been five months since his daughter's birth. He took his time heading back toward Florida, stopping to visit a couple of friends on the way. His first stop in Florida was in Tallahassee, where Ralph was attending Florida State University.

He could always talk to his brother, and he spent two days confiding in him and basically offloading many of the thoughts and ideas that comprised his mental being at the time. Ralph had a daughter named Laurie who was born four months after Don's daughter, Leigh. It was not lost on Don that his brother's attitude on parenthood was obviously far different from his own. There had been some similarities surrounding the births of their respective children.

Don had taken Ralph and his wife, Gay, out to dinner, since they were struggling under the GI Bill while in school. Plastic money was being used to finance his trip, so why not share his artificial wealth.

Continuing his trip, he spent three days visiting with old classmates at the University of Florida in Gainesville.

The following day Don found himself making the one phone call that he was allowed. He informed his parents that he was in jail in Daytona Beach. Picked up for vagrancy, the police had run a check and found out that the Bank of America was looking for both his car and his card. The charges were minor and his bail was low, but he was broke by then.

His parents called Ralph, who drove that evening from Tallahassee to Daytona and bailed him out. Ralph had also loaned him the money to catch the Greyhound for those final miles to West Palm Beach. He remembered thinking that it hadn't taken his brother long to pay back the favor of dinner.

Back in West Palm, he kicked around with no real purpose except to have a good time. A job collecting change from pool tables and other vending machines located in bars and restaurants gave him access to many of the local watering holes.

Some months later, Rachel brought Don's daughter to visit her grandparents. Seeing Rachel again rekindled those feelings that had attracted him to her when they first met. Away from California, they both thought that perhaps their relationship had a chance. Rachel, too, had been stirred by her feelings for this person who had swept into her life less than two years ago. They reconciled and soon found an apartment.

Don had realized that a college degree was an asset, and he was less than two years away from attaining the necessary credits to graduate. He

24

couldn't let his brother get one up on him by having the only college degree in the family. Rachel not only had encouraged him, but she actually got together the necessary transcripts and information to enroll him at Florida Atlantic University in Boca Raton. FAU was still a new school. It only had an upper division consisting of juniors and seniors.

The honeymoon between him and Rachel only lasted a few months. It was apparent, after this second attempt, that Don was just not the domestic type. The relationship ended and she walked out on him after he broke her nose with an open handed slap. This was the only time that he had ever struck her, but the message to Rachel was clear. She still cared for him, but her own strong will would not tolerate a life role with her being cast as the victim.

For his part, Don regretted striking her, but maybe not as much as he should have. This loss of control was destined to be repeated in subsequent relationships. What caused him to exhibit this type of behavior? There was no exposure to it during his childhood, and he had never cared for bullies. It was like a thunderstorm slowly gathering up warm air and pushing it aloft, until a difference in electrical charges resulted in a sudden release of energy, a black cloud that seemed to form over any meaningful association with a person of the opposite sex. Thunderstorms were a common occurrence in the tropics, and Don lived in the tropics. Strangely, Don respected Rachel for walking out on him. Not so much at the time, but over the years, when he observed how much abuse many other women were willing to suffer before throwing in the towel.

HIS EDUCATIONAL GOAL NOW was to take the path of least resistance, and that seemed to be a degree in physical education, which could lead to a teaching job. Don was in excellent shape and had participated in gymnastics while at the academy. His dad had been a coach in the service, so this was an easy fit. He zoomed through school while working part-time and utilizing the GI Bill for additional support. There was still time to dive. He developed a new circle of friends and renewed links with older friends still in the area. A job at another ranch managed to keep him in spending money, while doing something that he really enjoyed. An old dune buggy, which he had purchased, allowed him to spend a lot of time cruising the beaches of northern Palm Beach and southern Martin Counties. The beaches were not built up at the time.

While interning as part of his degree requirements, he realized that the newly integrated schools were not going to be part of his future. He just didn't have the tolerance for the lack of discipline condoned by the school system. His own short fuse would put him at risk in dealing with students who had disciplinary problems. He didn't want to be a part of the transition through which local schools were going.

As graduation approached, most of his classmates were preoccupied with searching for jobs; however, Don had already determined that he was not going to need a resume. He had been busy networking for the past year. His contacts included people in every strata of the boating community. He had talked to and befriended everyone from hardworking fisherman to hardly working yacht owners.

Don already knew that his future included boats on the bouncing waves of the sea and not balls bouncing on school playgrounds. The irony that earning a degree from Florida Atlantic better prepared him for a life on the sea than earning a degree from the U.S. Naval Academy was not lost on him.

∽ CHAPTER THREE ∽

"The things we collect in our modern life
Come heaped with boundless responsibility.
And as they entwine us, so comes the strife;
Lost in the process is so much possibility."

AUTHOR

DON LOOKED UP. The two Swiss girls were gone. Oh well! This was his turf and he knew for sure that their paths would cross again. After all, this was a fairly isolated spot on a rather small island.

Where was he? As he drifted back into his thoughts, he was quickly drawn to where he had left off in this life review. Reflection seemed to be the dominant activity on this particular morning.

A vision of a newly graduated twenty-five-year-old arriving in West End on Grand Bahama Island made him aware that he was once again rehashing his past.

He had managed to hitch a ride on a yacht that had departed West Palm bound for West End. This sixty-five-mile trip had the same effect as a voyage into outer space. He had arrived in another world. His minimal baggage consisted of: an Igloo brand cooler stuffed with clothes, a half-filled sea bag, a couple of Hawaiian slings, and a spear gun.

It was a stroke of good fortune when he crossed paths with a local white Bahamian by the name of Kevin. Kevin was about Don's age, and unlike many of his fellow Bahamians, he loved to dive. The fear of the water that many Bahamians felt always puzzled Don. Their mutual love of diving was the catalyst that led to a bond between these two young men of such different backgrounds. The pursuit of ladies was another interest that they shared. Kevin's father had wanted him to join the family liquor business, but Kevin opted to start his own venture with Don as his partner. Since it was virtually impossible at that time for a U.S. citizen to get a work permit, Donnie's participation as a partner was based on a handshake. He was truly a silent partner, at least as far as any paperwork was concerned.

The two went into the diving business, or maybe it would be more accurate to say the fishing business. They began to supply local hotels and restaurants between West End and Freeport with fish. Each morning they would free dive for various fish and lobster until they had filled a fifty-gallon drum sufficiently to meet that day's orders. Diving for as long as it took, they would never catch more than they had sold.

Donnie did not view this as a job, and he became very sensitive if you referred to what he did as *work*. Kevin took care of the paperwork, and Donnie relied on Kevin's integrity for determining how the money was divided. If they reached their daily quota early, they would often spend time exploring their underwater hunting grounds. Their workplace had been well decorated by Mother Nature. Like many people who work outdoors in a natural setting, they did not have to wait until the end of a year to receive their bonuses.

They soon earned a reputation for their diving prowess. Both were able to stay down for prolonged periods without having to come up for air. When they had first started, scuba tanks were used to supply oxygen, but they soon shed those. Refilling and charging tanks was a logistical nightmare. The tanks simply slowed them down. Diving without tanks, or *free diving*, as it was better known, allowed them to maximize their time in the water and to minimize their time in the boat fussing with gear. Often, the two would compete to see who could dive the deepest and/or stay down the longest.

Scuba diving had not achieved the level of popularity that it now has, and red and white dive flags had not proliferated in those waters. Soon, locals, as well as visitors to West End, were spreading stories that had as their origin the diving exploits of Don and Kevin.

Visiting boaters would attempt to ingratiate themselves with Donnie in the hopes that he might show them some pretty reefs or put them on reefs containing fish or lobsters. Frequently, one reef satisfied both criteria.

His recall of this period was so vivid that Don felt he had been transported back in time. It was as if he was living those days once more. They had been very happy days, so it was not abnormal for him to rehash them with such ardor.

Mixing another drink, he hoped for a smooth transition back to the time in his reflections. Mixing drinks had become a natural act, almost a habit. Reflection, though, was not a habit at this stage in his life, but the reverie had been so vivid that it had overcome him.

In a little more than a year, Donnie's diving skills had separated him from the pack. Attainment of those skills had given him an identity that he took great pride in, and he was very conscious of fostering, as well as protecting, his reputation.

On the warm nights that blessed this part of the world so often, he began honing another skill to augment his reputation as a diver. Womanizing was an area that did not come quite as naturally as diving. After a couple of drinks though, his natural gift of gab combined with the mood of the Islands was usually sufficient for him to achieve some level of success.

He was not one to talk about his accomplishments, so the reputation he earned in this area took more time to develop. However, West End was a small community and other people did notice. These people were not under the same gag order that bound Donnie as a gentleman. How did women hear about Don? A few tactful inquiries, who knows! He exuded

A Victim of Some of That Energy

29

energy, and maybe there was some correlation between that energy and the magnetism that attracts people to one another.

BAHAMIAN LAW PROHIBITED AN INDIVIDUAL from spending more than six months in the Islands without an interruption. This meant that Don had to return stateside from time to time.

On return trips, he would stay at his mother's house, but this was not his first choice. A short visit was long enough. They would exchange pleasantries, and Don would provide her assistance with such things as making repairs, or more often than not, recommending someone for the job. His mother kept a bedroom for him. Her house was like a bed and breakfast inn, but the primary guest was usually out.

Then he remembered meeting Judy one evening. Their lifestyles seemed to mesh. She made him welcome at her place whenever he returned to Florida. He enjoyed her company, and she enjoyed his, unless he overindulged, at which point, he could be abusive. Her duplex provided a base of operations, and Don was an operator. His normal mode of transportation at this time was a bicycle.

On these return trips to the states, he usually had money in his pockets. Actually, he carried his money separately, since he rarely wore anything that even had pockets. He loved volleyball and would always look for a game. The games that he found during the week were normally played at night, as most people were working.

Don would often hang out at the beach during the day. There, he was in his element. He would minimize his exposure to the sun and heat of the day by finding refuge at the Beer Barrel Pub. This little tavern was located about sixty yards from the sands of Riviera Beach. It was a popular watering hole for locals of diverse backgrounds.

Donnie enjoyed playing tennis at the public courts, which were located just in front of this strategically situated little bar. This was the Bath and Tennis Club of the *working class*. Well actually, there was no bath. You had to use the public showers at the beach before retiring to the Beer Barrel for shooters and cold draft beer.

The Beer Barrel was Donnie's office. He took calls there and retrieved his messages from his secretary who was the on duty barmaid, usually Annie. His circle of friends included bankers, businessmen, attorneys, construction workers, commercial fishermen, and the unemployed. He could move effortlessly from a conversation on the gross national product, to yesterday's gross take of lobsters, to the gross injustices of life, to the gross topless dancer of the previous evening.

The Beer Barrel was the planning and staging area for many a foray. Most of these forays were in the pursuit of fun, but Don was aware of an undercurrent of plots of a more devious nature.

An afternoon of socializing would often stretch into the evening. Don would then hop on his bike and head for Judy's apartment. The amount of alcohol that he had consumed usually had a bearing on how well he was received by his hostess. On many occasions, he found himself in a maudlin state. When this happened, he was painfully aware that he did not have a good grip on his drinking.

His dad's drinking problem had bothered him when he was younger. Excessive consumption of alcohol had been the source of many a fight between him and his dad. He used to recoil at the smell of stale beer. A foul odor would permeate the house on many mornings. It emanated from a half-full or a half-empty, depending on your viewpoint, glass that graced the table next to his dad's favorite chair—the chair where his dad had fallen asleep while watching TV. It was an almost predictable end to his father's day. His father, with so much potential, had wasted most of the gifts bestowed on him at birth. Had this curse of alcohol addiction been passed on to Don, or was it a lack of closure with his dad's death that led him to acquire this personality trait? Didn't psychologists have a theory for this?

He disdained the results that a close relationship with a bottle could have on a person. The problem, Don realized, was that he didn't think

31

*A Rare Use of Scuba Gear Yields
Three Good Sized Lobsters*

about this when having his first drink of the day. He only thought of it after too many drinks. Of course, he was young and could stop drinking should his own problem persist.

Don would soon tire from this stateside routine, as he would tire from routine in general. The Bahamas had a strong pull on him. His ever-vigilant network of contacts would soon produce a ride back to the islands.

A benefactor, who ferried him to the islands, would be promptly compensated. The currency of exchange was fish or lobster tails. When Don returned a favor, the slate was cleared with the person involved, usually owing Don.

MANY YACHT OWNERS, planning to do more extensive traveling in the Bahamas, would ask Donnie to join them. He more than carried his weight, if for no other reason than the security that he provided the respective boat owner. This process worked well for Don. It enabled him to see more of the islands that he loved so much. It gave him access to diving spots that might not otherwise have been available, all of this in the comfort of someone else's yacht. He didn't have to worry about repairs, or fuel, or food. He was unencumbered and, in his mind, free to enjoy time to its fullest.

No cruise like this was undertaken with someone whom he did not initially like. Some of these cruises, however, would bring out flaws in people that were not apparent in a casual relationship. These faults could appear in either party.

Those who understood Don's quick temper and could work around it were often rewarded with diving or life experiences that would be

32

permanently etched in their memories. Don, for his part, worked hard on improving his low tolerance for ineptitude in any form. The more that he liked what the other person was made of, the more apt he was to overlook their nautical shortcomings.

Over time, he became an advocate of the rule —of: *if there is no harm then there is no foul.* His interpretation of the rule was, if you wanted to screw up your boat or your self, that was fine, just don't damage another person's property or his body.

As a temporary member of a vessel's crew, he brought another trait to the boat. His gift of conversation was probably passed on to him from his dad's gene pool. This trait was honed over many evenings of sitting at anchor, wiling away the hours without the assistance of television. Conversation was what people resorted to for purposes of entertainment. Don's high level of intelligence enabled him to converse with all manner of people. It did not matter what your background or station in life was. When you conversed with Don, he did not talk up or talk down to you. He looked you directly in the eye, and you knew that you were on an even keel for that moment.

When first meeting Don, it was not unusual for a person to brand him as a hippie. That was a major mistake. Yes, Don had long hair, and yes, he wore sandals, and yes, he smoked a little pot, but these superficial similarities ended once you got inside his head.

Hippies tended to be classified as non-conformists, sort of in your face, anti-society types. Many, not all, were more interested in being different, just for the shock value. Their communes and way of life offered an alternative to a regimented, overly governed society. The problem was that they were never able to advance their agenda, due to a lack of inertia, brought on by smoke induced stagnation and the pursuit of pleasure. Some good ideas died by the poppy-seeded, LSD-strewn wayside.

Don, on the other hand, was more of an individualist in search of adventure. He was more a conservative than a liberal. He was not out to change anything. He wore rubber sandals because his feet were always getting wet, and he grew a beard because he didn't like to shave with saltwater, and very few people described him as mellow. The pursuit of pleasure was something he had in common with his hippie friends. He had met and befriended many counterculturists who were traveling in the Islands, usually on older sailboats.

Don was sensitive, though, and he did not like to be typecast as a hippie. "Speedo," when it showed, was the only label he wore.

∽ CHAPTER FOUR ∽

Penetrating the depths, diving free,
Marks a trip beneath the waves with intensity.
Concentrating and focusing on the sights below,
Limited air serves to enhance Nature's undersea show.

With oxygen waning, you strain to last,
Back to the surface means back to the past.
There is no rush to resurface; what's up above,
Storms and turbulence and unfulfilled love?

AUTHOR

VERY FEW INDIVIDUALS, if any, could claim to have made as many dives in the pursuit of fish and lobster as Don did during those years.

The sheer number of dives, in and of itself, was bound to have led to some dangerous incidents. Incidents did occur, even though Don tried to minimize them. His stubbornness and persistence were often the cause of situations that put him in peril.

For example, he once speared a large jewfish. His aim wasn't perfect, so the fish still did not consider itself dead. It began to dive with Don's spear still attached. Don could not afford to lose the spear, so he hung on. Since he was free diving, his time was limited. The contest between life for the fish and the spear ended with Don reaching the surface after what seemed an eternity to his diving partner, who was on the boat. He was gasping for air, but his spear and his pride were both intact. His partner could not believe that a person was capable of staying down that long, especially while exerting himself as Don had done.

Don had been attacked several times by barracudas while bringing speared fish to the surface. Usually, the barracuda was after the fish impaled on his spear. It was sometimes hard to tell exactly whom the barracuda's target was when he darted. There was often less than a foot between fingers and fins (Don's fingers and the fins of the bleeding fish on his spear). The hand that he used to hold the spear had been bitten at least three times by these extremely quick silver torpedoes with their warheads of sharp teeth. On more than one occasion, Don could have avoided peril by dropping the spear, but that was not his style.

His hands also bore the scars of several encounters with moray eels. This was an occupational hazard of the lobster hunting trade. If a lobster were cornered in a hole, he would often stick his spear under the coral and prod his quarry out into the open. Often, another lobster hunter would be lurking under the reef. Morays do not like to share their hunting grounds, or maybe they, too, felt cornered by Don. In either case, they attacked his hand and his wrist on at least ten occasions. It was his right hand and wrist that bore the scars. These wounds would lead to a loss of blood, and Don certainly didn't like being near blood in the water, whether it was his or a fish's. These wounds, almost always, required stitches when he got back into port.

His body also bore a few scratches from sharks' teeth. He hunted sharks with what he called a bang stick. This was a spear rigged with a detonating device that was designed to go off on contact. The ammunition was a slug-type, shotgun shell. He would approach to within a few feet of the predator. Then, he would place the spear point, ideally, as close to the shark's head as possible. The shock of the shell going off and or the penetration of the slug were usually sufficient to kill it instantly. Getting that close to his prey did not always go smoothly. Don never felt that a shark had actually attacked him; however, several had come close enough to brush against him. It was his feeling that this was just accidental contact, which occurred as they took evasive action to avoid him. Several small sharks had attempted to take fish away from him, fish that were still on his spear. In the wrestling match that ensued, his skin had come in contact with their teeth. None of these bites proved serious. This was similar to the barracuda attacks, but in these instances, he never felt the sharks were after him.

The Jaw of One of Those Sharks

Initially, he had hunted sharks for sport. After collecting several impressive sets of jaws, his better sense told him that maybe this was interfering with the balance of the underwater environment. He never hunted sharks again, unless a good and specific reason to do so presented itself.

His knowledge of sharks was impressive enough to land him a temporary job. A movie company hired him to protect one of their stars from a shark attack during the filming of a sequence shot in the Atlantic. Of course, this was an adventure for Don, and he did not consider it to be a job. The star survived the filming with all his limbs, and Don added another notch on the totem pole that represented his life.

THE OCEAN WAS A GREAT ADVENTURE GROUND FOR DON. Even before cocaine came into his life, he was snorting through his nose. The substance that he ingested in those earlier years was salt spray, and it gave him an immense high. When he was snorting salt spray, it meant that he was communing with his first love. The ocean brought him so much pleasure.

It wasn't necessary for him to be beneath the water in order to enjoy it. He was one of the early devotees of the sport of windsurfing. The sail of his windsurfer could be seen heading out of the inlet by the socialites who lived in Palm Beach. The colorful sail was also visible to the throngs of the less affluent who dotted the sands of Riviera Beach. His board skimmed the oft-churned waters of the Intracoastal Highway and the smoother waters that surrounded many of the Bahamian Isles. As was the case on his boat, Don preferred to windsurf au natural.

37

He would share his knowledge of windsurfing with anyone who was interested. This skill had not been learned from a book, but rather gained through much personal experience. Don's lifestyle afforded him the opportunity to spend countless hours pursuing whatever pastime happened to catch his fancy. Don would spend time teaching individuals to windsurf if they were genuinely interested. He might be slightly more patient with his female students, but his patience would soon wear thin if the student did not show improvement.

Don possessed an underlying desire to teach any of the skills in life that he had acquired. There was one catch: he was best suited for teaching advanced students, students who brought something to the table in the way of mental or physical acumen. You did not have to be both smart and physical for him to like you; however, it helped if you were gifted with at least one of those traits. Florida Atlantic University had given him a degree in teaching, but that degree would never dictate what forum he would teach in or who Don would select for his students. The traditional bell curve was not a consideration in his selection process. Just as many employers will show a preference for veterans when filling open positions, Don would show a preference for young, pretty girls when it came to selecting students for his school of random skills. He was quite liberal with his definition of pretty, and as he got older, he expanded his definition of young. In fact, he was probably at the forefront of consciousness with regard to age

38

discrimination. He taught countless people to handle a boat, dive, windsurf, play volleyball, play backgammon, fillet fish, extract conch meat, etc.

These were only a few of the skills taught in his classroom without walls. There was no tuition for his school. If you wanted to give something in return that was fine, but not necessary. This was one of the reasons Don liked to include females in his normally one-on-one classes. Women had a way of showing their appreciation for his teachings that he very much enjoyed (the barter system working to perfection, with all debts canceled and no long-term contracts).

Don's love for the water was not confined to the sea alone. Fresh water activities held a strong allure for him. In Maine, on a very cold Schoodic Lake, he had learned to ride a wooden surfboard pulled behind a small boat by a straining 10 HP engine. This was long before the invention of wave boards built of lightweight composites. The slow speed of the boat required the rider to create a minimal drag. It was always an adventure to keep the board straight as you attempted to extricate yourself from the cold water. Success meant that you could speed along at a brisk ten miles an hour, dripping wet in the cold air.

Don graduated to water skis and then to a slalom ski in the warmer waters of Lake Osborne, which was located just south of West Palm Beach. He really enjoyed slalom skiing, but he was always at the mercy of some friend who had a fast enough boat. An independent cuss, he didn't like being at anyone's mercy, so most of his waterskiing was done later in life, when he owned his own boat.

Water in the form of snow was fine too. He had always enjoyed sledding. His brief exposure to snow, as a child, came when living in Maine and in Colorado.

While back from the islands on one of his government mandated, semi-annual departures, he had accepted an invitation by his brother to go snow skiing in Colorado. Neither he nor his brother had ever skied before. An opportunity to try this sport occurred when a friend of his brother's had offered free lodging near Arapaho, otherwise known as "Big A Basin." Both

Don and His Brother on a Skiing Expedition

had learned to ski with minimal instructions from his brother's friend. The natural competitive fires between them had been lit. It might not have been pretty, but they both persevered, and they were soon racing each other down the mountain. After several falls, they declared a truce and actually helped each other while skiing together in a harmonious, non-competitive manner (if you could call flailing skis and tumbling skiers harmonious). When the trip ended five days later, Don had added another water sport to his collection.

He subsequently took two more ski trips with his brother to Squaw Valley and Tahoe. On the trip to Tahoe, several of his brother's friends had joined them. Don had marveled at how the group would go out of their way for the $1.99 breakfasts and then lose fifty dollars while waiting for it to be served. The friends marveled at how Don would come all that way to go skiing and then take an afternoon off to visit the Mustang Ranch. It certainly wasn't Don's love of horses that motivated him to leave the snow and head for the valley floor below. It must have been his love of cowgirls. The group shared some laughs when Don described his adventures. He bartered with the girls at the brothel, offering some illicit substance that he had brought along in return for their favors. Based on his account of the tale, the guys guessed that he was a hit.

He also decided to go skiing in the Alps. This trip, undertaken alone, proved to be a disappointment. The language barrier and the high cost of being there left an ugly impression. Any further contacts with Europeans would take place on his home turf.

THOSE WHO DID NOT KNOW DON very well sometimes drew the conclusion that he was a bigot. What these people concluded to be bigotry was not

40

bigotry in the classical sense. He may have been intolerant, but it was not racially or politically motivated. It was his low tolerance for ineptness in people that others often confused for bigotry. Don could probably be better described as particular. His wrath would unleash in an instant, no matter who you were, if you made a mistake at what he deemed to be a critical moment, especially as it related to boating. You did not want to mishandle a line when approaching a dock nor did you want to violate any of the rules of good seamanship.

One day, a good attorney friend of his made the mistake of dropping an anchor before the boat had slowed to a stop. He told Don later: he would much rather face an exacting judge than be tongue whipped by him again. Despite that incident, their friendship remained intact.

Many native Bahamians were included in his list of friends. He was able to keep these islanders on his list by minimizing the possibility of their being involved in a critical moment with him. Many other non-Bahamians, whose company he enjoyed, were never allowed into his life deeply enough for them to share a critical moment. This was his way of preserving a relationship. If you didn't put a person in a position to screw up, they wouldn't. However, the people that Don really cared for had to pay the price of constant scrutiny. Most people could not stand up to this scrutiny and they either dropped out of his life or remained on the periphery.

Those who could tolerate this constant analysis were the ones who knew Don the best. They took him for what he was, a free spirit, and that freedom brought a ray of hope to those who toiled in a more confined lifestyle.

Where had the morning gone? Don did not realize how long he had spent re-exploring the past. He was not one to defer the pleasures of the present. The two Swiss girls had not reappeared. Don stood up and did a quick survey of his habitat. Don was not your normal Habitat for Humanity sort of guy; however, he was into mending fences, and he did owe the two Swiss prospects an apology. He decided to seek them out and ask for forgiveness. How could he have ignored two such beautiful women?

First though, he dropped to the deck and did three sets of thirty push-ups. He followed with fifty sit-ups. This was enough to break a sweat. As the alcohol leached from his body, he began to feel more like joining the rest of the world, at least for now. All of this activity did not go unnoticed. He strolled to the outdoor shower at the end of the dock. No sooner was he finished drying off, then who should appear, but the two, European honeys. What a coincidence! Soon all three were engaged in an animated conversation. The girls used gestures to complement their broken English. Don used gestures to dramatize his speech. He was not trained in the theater, but he had been quick to learn that gesticulating seemed to add to his powers of persuasion. The fact that the girls just happened to show up at this time meant he would not need to be very persuasive. Inga and Marie arranged to meet Don in an hour for a ride on the Robalo.

The only illicit cargo that his faded yellow boat carried that day was the thoughts that went through Don's mind. These thoughts were no longer of the past. His mind was now concentrating on the future, the near future.

The waters around Treasure Cay provided a perfect backdrop for a "passion play," and Donnie definitely planned to make his play. He was content, though, to show off his backyard first. The girls had only viewed this paradise from the beach. Out on the water, their eyes were confronted with a totally different vista. Don sensed what they were experiencing, a sensation that had brought him to this lifestyle in the first place.

On a day like this, the ocean was far from threatening. It was not awful. It was awe striking. No matter how often he had plied these waters, Don still took pleasure from his surroundings. The water was crystal clear. The sky was lightly sprinkled with small cumulus clouds, and the low islands, which dotted the horizon, provided the contrast. Don waited patiently for the state of relaxation that typically followed the sensory overload. There would be no popping of fuses. Instead, people just seemed to slip slowly into a state of relaxation. Any tension present at the start of the day drowned under this watery paradise.

Inga and Marie were on vacation, so they were not under much tension. They had wholeheartedly embraced the rules of the boat, and they were sitting naked near the bow. Something to quench the thirst, a couple of drinks (Don never left port without his cooler), and the mood on the boat became quite laid-back. Well, the girls were laid-back, but Captain Don was lying back (lying back and waiting for the moment). He had been here before, and was confident that physical pleasures would soon be his.

Donnie liked European women. They seemed less inhibited than their American counterparts, and were more prone to sexual experimentation. Donnie certainly didn't consider himself a scientist, but he did believe in the scientific method. Gathering empirical data on women's sexual likes and dislikes was more like a hobby for him.

The thoughts on Don's mind began to physically express themselves. He noticed the girls were looking his way and giggling. They were not looking at his face. His thoughts had congregated, somewhat, lower on his body, and it was apparent that he was quite a thoughtful person. Donnie cut the engine, and made his way toward the bow. He reached for the boat's anchor, and Inga and Marie reached for his anchor. An hour later the three of them decided that a swim would be a nice way to cool their bodies and rinse off the traces of their passions.

They all donned goggles, flippers, and snorkels for a leisurely swim around the shallow reef below. Getting back into the boat, Don stopped for a moment to watch the water glisten as it ran off the naked bodies of his two passengers. This was Don's idea of going down to the sea in ships. He was not the son of a son of a sailor man, but he sure did like the water, especially when it cascaded off a nude woman's breasts.

43

Once on the boat, the trio dried each other off. Drinks were in order, and they were soon sipping on plain orange juice in lieu of a screwdriver, which was the normal beverage of choice. Donnie's adherence to healthy drinking dictated that he mix his alcohol with either orange juice or cranberry juice. These mixers held scurvy at bay, but the vodka could cause scurviness.

The trio opted to take a few hits of the substance that Don transported from time to time. After a couple of tokes, Don lamented to the girls about his trip to the Alps. Why had he gone to the Austrian Alps when there was such pleasure lurking in the Swiss Alps? The girls countered by telling him you could not sit out in the mountains back in Switzerland during the winter with your body bare for very long. Not one to encumber his body with clothes, he agreed with the girls that, perhaps, this might have influenced his opinion of the Alps.

The conversation soon turned to the subject of contrast. Didn't contrast heighten one's life experiences? Didn't you more fully appreciate the moment when you could compare it to a wide range of other moments? Or did you take away from the present moment by comparing it with previous ones? What about those who were doomed to lead sheltered lives because of economic disadvantage? Were their opportunities to experience a wide range of moments limited? A lively discussion concluded that contrast was relative. Hence, any person could experience contrast, and it was important that they did, in order to bring enhanced meaning to their lives. Make a conscious effort not to get in a rut. Ruts are by definition lacking in contrast.

Contrast at this time called for a change in the depth of the conversation. Don tried to lighten the mood with a couple of jokes, but they lost something in the translation. A true test of the mastery of another person's language is how well you grasp their humor. Inga and Marie may not have caught the jokes, but they did have a sense of humor, and Don was able to keep them laughing with his mannerisms.

The afternoon sea breeze began to wane as it usually did with the approach of evening, so they hoisted the anchor. On the trip back to the marina, they decided to meet later for drinks and dinner and whatever else might follow.

After a short nap and a shower, Donnie was ready for round two. Round two ended that evening back on the *Oar Dog*, with Don down for the count. Another sexual interlude with both girls had convinced him that there would be no round three. Satisfying two women, such as Inga and Marie, was both exhilarating and exhausting. Two very happy Swiss ladies boarded the plane for the trip home the next morning.

Don Inspecting His Domain

⁓ CHAPTER FIVE ⁓

"I've always wanted to travel afar,
But the cost to do so seems extreme.
Worries about future security
Limit the scope of even my dreams.
Let me reach deep down inside
And grasp for the currents that let me glide."

AUTHOR

ALTHOUGH IT WAS NOT ALWAYS APPARENT, Don strove to keep balance in his life. Since he led a non-traditional lifestyle, his balancing act was not readily apparent.

His brother had found this out a few years back in January of 1977. When he found out that Ralph had left his job, sold his house, and bought a sailboat, Don was both surprised and worried. Ralph had a good job, a nice house, three kids, and a wife. What was his brother thinking? He knew that, like himself, Ralph was comfortable around the water, but Don was also aware that his only sibling was totally lacking in sailing knowledge. Worse yet, Ralph was planning a trip to the Islands.

January was the month during which Don normally balanced his drinking habit. Don reasoned that if he could go the whole month without a drink, then he was not alcohol dependent. For the last six years, January had been a dry month for him. Since his brother's planned trip coincided with his annual period of fasting, why not give his brother a hand? Of

47

course, Ralph had not asked, but what the hell, it was the brotherly thing to do. Besides, there was his niece and two nephews to think about as well as Ralph's wife, Gay. He wasn't sure about Gay. She was always cordial and friendly, but he had the feeling that she didn't approve of the way that he treated the women in his life.

That particular year, January had been a horrible month, weather-wise. Ralph had tried twice to start for the Islands and had to turn back both times (once because of the weather and a second time because of equipment failure). While sitting at anchor, waiting for a third attempt, Ralph awakened to a howling wind that broadcasted the arrival of an impending front. What made this front different was the snow that Ralph viewed from his porthole. Going topside, he was greeted by choppy waves in what was normally a tranquil anchorage, south of Peanut Island. This was the only time on record that it had snowed in Palm Beach. The snowfall was short in duration, but it would be long in the memories of those who witnessed it.

Against that backdrop, Don suddenly appeared with his offer to crew for the trip across the Gulf Stream. Ralph had, subsequently, confessed that he felt a higher being had sent Don. Two evenings later, the *Yutaka*, a thirty-three foot trimaran, was on its way across the Gulf Stream. Don had limited sailing experience on a boat of this size, but he understood the dynamics of the wind from his countless days of windsurfing.

At Don's suggestion, they left at nightfall. The strategy was to reach West End in the daylight, since the Bahamian navigational markers left a little to be desired. It was a windy night, and about halfway through the trip, the mainsail blew out with a loud whoosh! They managed to lower what remained of the sail, and continued the trip using the mizzen and the storm jib. Even with reduced sail, they had reached the tip of the Bahamian bank just before daylight. They were north of their intended destination and only a quick tack kept them from running aground on a shallow reef. Don's instincts had saved the day when, despite the poor light, he had detected the color change in the water that indicated shoaling. Two

Yutaka *(Ralph's Boat)*

hours later Donnie was introducing Ralph to the officials that manned the docks at West End. There was some pride in his voice. He did give his brother high marks for the composure that he had displayed on the rather eventful crossing.

Normally, he would celebrate the conclusion of a voyage with a few drinks, but it was still January. Don was still concerned about Ralph and his family's ability to manage while cruising the Islands, so he offered to spend a little more time teaching them some of the nuances of diving for fish and lobster, cleaning conch, and other pearls of wisdom that he thought might help them. This was the teaching side of Don, and it came naturally.

The kids had been particularly interested when he had shown them how to extract the pistil from a conch and then to eat this slimy mass raw. He had told the boys that it would improve their virility. They were only six and seven at the time, but they got the idea. Ralph's ten-year-old daughter, Laurie, was a good student, and she seemed particularly attentive when he showed them how to break off the whip of a lobster and use it to remove the intestines.

Now, it had been some time since Don had partaken of alcohol, and he was getting a little surly. He was aware of the tension that his presence, on such a small boat with six people aboard, was causing. How had he passed the psychological screening for submarine school? He was sure that

49

his brother, an ex-submarine sailor was wondering the same thing. In the interest of family harmony, it was decided, on arriving at Walker's Cay, that it might be a good time for Don to jump ship. Ralph and his family seemed to agree and thanked him profusely for his help. They had parted with no hard feelings, and Don had meant it when he told Ralph that he respected him for the way that he was raising his family. The trip had given Don an opportunity to balance his nomadic existence.

IT WAS SEVERAL MONTHS LATER. Don looked out the window of the house that he had been caretaking for some friends just in time to see Ralph anchoring his boat in the tiny harbor. The anchorage at Saddle Cay, which was located north of Norman's Cay in the Exumas, was at capacity. It only took one boat to fill the small harbor. He had half expected the *Yutaka*, and was silently pleased that his brother had made it this far down into the Islands. Maybe they had heeded some of the advice that he had dispensed. Actually, Ralph had gone further south than the Exumas, and he was, in fact, on his way north again.

Don's companion at the time was a young blonde lady by the name of Patricia. Her stage name was Pretty Patty, and the stages that she normally graced had runways. She was not a model, however. Her main source of income was dollar bills stuffed in her garters. The patrons who watched her perform could have cared less about her show business aspirations. They just wanted to see her tits and whatever else she would bare. There was a direct relationship between the dollars she earned and the flesh that she displayed. Donnie, benefactor that he was, had rescued her from a downward spiral with drugs. There were no garters for him to stuff, and since she was part of his crew, she wore nada. She may not have been intellectually stimulating, but she sure could arouse other interests.

There were no supermarkets in this part of the world, and Don was running short of some basic food items. To resolve this temporary outage, they attached Don's little runabout to the back of *Yutaka*, and set sail for Nassau.

Before heading north to Nassau, Don had motored his skiff south to

50

Norman's Cay to make a phone call. This was shortly before the drug cartel had taken over the island and discouraged any visits by outsiders.

Patricia, in deference to the boys, covered her normally naked body with a skimpy little outfit. His nephews, as young as they were, spent more time looking at Pretty Patty's treasures than the treasures that lurked below the surface, the surface of the water, that is. Normally they would have been looking for starfish with six or four tentacles, but not on this day. Patricia was aware of their attention, and soon had them engaged in conversation. She was able to communicate at their level very well, and from the boy's point of view, it was a stimulating conversation. Don's niece Laurie watched silently. This was her first chance to observe the impact that one sex can have on the other in such a natural setting.

It was a beautiful day, and the wind was behind them. The day went well, as they successfully worked their way through the scattered underwater fields of coral heads. The seven of them took turns sitting near the bow, watching for these protrusions of coral. The chances were slim that they would hit one, but if this did occur, it would have certainly ruined the day, as well as the trip in general.

There is almost always something, either real or imagined, to ruin a perfect day. Perhaps that is why there are so few perfect days. The event that put a damper on this perfect day was real. Just three hundred yards from their intended anchorage, and while passing underneath the bridge to Paradise Island, the outboard motor on the trailing dinghy worked itself loose and sank to the bottom. The cable, which should have prevented this, parted from internal rust. The water at this point was about fifty feet deep. Don noted the spot, and after anchoring *Yutaka* in the harbor, he and Ralph returned on Don's skiff. Fifty feet was a piece of cake. It only took a short time to locate the motor resting on the bottom. With a line in his hand, Don swam to the bottom, attached it, and returned to the surface. Ralph, meanwhile, raised the motor and placed it on the skiff. After a thorough cleaning, it sputtered back to life, the same way a drowning person sputters when revived.

51

With Leigh

The recipient of the phone call that Don had placed earlier, while on Norman's Cay, arrived in Nassau the following day. It was his daughter, Leigh, now a bubbly ten year old. She had come for the weekend, and her dad tried to make it as memorable for her as it was meaningful for him.

He was awkward in the role of a father, but this was his daughter, and he loved her. Don just didn't show his love in the conventional ways. Leigh's dad would never be conventional, and she would just have to pay attention for the little signs that he gave her, the signs that indicated how he felt deep below the surface, because he was a "free diver," and free divers sputtered at the surface.

With Leigh on a plane back to her mother, Don and Patricia were on the way back to Saddle Cay, after having made plans with Ralph to rendezvous a couple of weeks later in the Berry Islands. Don knew that he could use the Islands' grapevine to determine his brother's whereabouts.

TWO WEEKS LATER, the stint as a house sitter ended when the couple, who normally held the job, returned from England. He had allowed Patricia the luxury of two coolers for storing her wardrobe, a regular forty-eight quart size for her clothes and a smaller six-pack size for her cosmetics. Surprisingly, this posed no problem, as Pretty Patty's clothing was scanty to begin with.

Most mariners would not use a fifteen-foot river skiff for transiting the various chains of islands that comprised the Bahamas. It was fine to scoot around the Exumas, the Berrys, or the Abacos in a boat this size, but it was definitely on the small side for making the ocean passages between the various chains.

Don overcame the handicap of traveling in a small boat by using his experience to choose the weather carefully. He headed north on the same

52

route that they had taken to Nassau two weeks earlier. After a couple of days of visiting friends in Nassau, he headed across thirty-four miles of open seas to Little Harbor in the Berrys. Little Harbor was located in about the center of a chain of islands that stretched for about ninety miles in a generally north to south direction. As always, he stopped to visit with acquaintances who were happy to receive him as a guest.

Three days later, he reached Great Harbor Cay, the largest of the islands that embodied the Berry chain. It was situated near the northern most tip of this archipelago.

He had stopped to spear a few fish on the way. Patricia was one of a series of ladies that Donnie had trained over the years to assist him with his diving. To qualify for this job, you needed to possess the requisite physical attributes, and you needed to be able to put up with his anger if you screwed up. Why would anyone apply? Well, if you did the job right, you would be the beneficiary of the magnetism and charm that drew women to Don in the first place.

His preferred method of diving was to attach a thirty-foot line to the back of his boat. With the boat moving at idle speed, Don would drag behind, holding the line with his left hand and his spear in his right hand. Wearing a mask and flippers and using a snorkel, he would scan the bottom in search of prey. Prey could be fish to order, any random, edible fish, or lobster. He compensated for less than perfect eyesight by tuning into his instincts. His ability to spot the movement of a lobster's whip as it receded underneath a coral ledge was uncanny. When he spotted his intended prey, he would let go of the line and swim below to gain position on his target. In the case of a fish, he usually tried to approach them at an angle from slightly behind or from above. Then he would wait for them to turn. At that second, they would be moving at their slowest relative rate. He would let fly his spear, which had been previously pulled back in the sling, as he neared the fish. In the case of lobsters, he would descend to their hole and attempt to confront them. He did not want his spear to penetrate the tail of the lobster. This was the edible portion of the crawfish, as lobsters are sometimes referred to in the Islands.

Now, this is where his mate had better be paying attention. Her job was to steer the general course that Don had prescribed, and to look back, frequently, for signals from his spear. He would raise his spear and point in the direction that he wanted to go based on what he saw below. The key was to respond at the moment that he released the line and dove. At that point, Patricia, in this case, had to turn back and circle the boat around the position where he had submerged. If this maneuver was executed properly, she would be close to Don when he surfaced. This was very important, because when he came gasping to the surface, he usually had a bleeding fish or a couple of lobsters skewered on his spear. Don was persnickety, and he did not like to be kept waiting while treading water. The sooner he could fling his catch into the boat, the better. He also did not like to alter his course to the surface in order to dodge the boat and its' still spinning props. With the prey in the boat, he would either dive the spot again or grab the line, and resume the search.

In a perfect world, Don would prefer to have two people towing behind the boat, but he was aware that the world was far from perfect, and so he compensated by going it alone, quite often. The first reason that two was better than one was that towing behind a boat made you look like bait being trolled through the water. This disturbance in the water occasionally attracted sharks and barracuda. So it was helpful to have someone watching your flank. The second reason was that it was nice to have someone watching your back while you were concentrating on tickling a lobster out of its hole. A third reason was that it just makes good sense to follow the buddy system whenever you are swimming. The fourth reason was that it was nice to have a witness to your underwater exploits. Who is going to tell the tales? Lastly, it gives you a comrade in arms to share a drink with when the diving is done.

The fish were presented to the dockmaster, a native Bahamian, at Bullocks Harbor. There were more than enough grouper and hogfish to exchange for the fuel that he needed. Yes, the dockmaster, Henry, had heard that there was a trimaran anchored in Bertram's Cove, a beautiful little indentation on the north shore of Great Stirrup Cay. Henry invited Don and Patricia to join him and his wife for dinner and to catch a shower at his modest little cottage. Don liked Henry and graciously accepted the invitation. When they departed the following morning, Henry's wife, Mary, was somewhat relieved. She liked Donnie, but she had caught Henry ogling Pretty Patty's anatomy a little more often than she liked.

AS DON ROUNDED THE BEND INTO BERTRAM'S COVE, he immediately spotted the *Yutaka*. There were only two boats in the harbor and the second boat, a twenty-eight-foot Cigarette, was rafted up to Ralph's boat. The Cigarette belonged to a prominent Pompano Beach dentist. The dentist, his stunning wife, his daughter, and another couple (Bill and his voluptuous wife, Peggy) were stranded when the boat's starter malfunctioned. They had just removed the starter, but they had a dilemma, the very dilemma that Don shunned like the plague: their boat had broken down in the Islands. Who does repairs, or where do you get repairs of this type done? Often, the answer lies on another island miles away or even back in the States.

Well, Don to the rescue. He at least knew where they needed to start. He unloaded Pretty Patty on the *Yutaka*, much to the delight of his nephews. Together with Ralph, Matt, the owner of the Cigarette, and Bill, his passenger, they headed back to Bullocks Harbor, which was several miles away on another island. Matt needed to be back the next day. There was a practice that required his attendance. Woe be it to any of his patients that might be in pain, because it was Matt that suffered the pain when he found out that it would be two days before a replacement part could be shipped in from Miami. This was the Islands, so pain medicine in the form of rum or beer was available, albeit at an inflated price. The four of them returned to the *Yutaka*, which had become their home base, feeling no pain.

The three boats, rafted together, did not form a very homogeneous mix, but the crews got along famously. You could spend a lot of time on the water without seeing a river skiff, a trimaran, and a Cigarette tied together (maybe at the Columbus Day Regatta in Biscayne Bay, but rarely anywhere else).

55

The combined crews of these vessels woke up one morning to a colorful display of beach umbrellas dotting the shore of the small harbor. Perplexed, they dinghied ashore to find out what the deal was. The answer was soon in coming. A blaring sound filled the air. Glancing seaward, they were shocked to see a huge cruise ship dropping anchor just outside the cove. In less than an hour, this previously uninhabited beach was the home of hundreds of tourists, complete with a band playing island music and a full-scale barbecue.

For Don and his brother this was a mixed blessing. They were welcomed as part of the local color, and were provided a rare opportunity to eat meat, but what had happened to this island paradise? They decided the price was too high, and they were not saddened to see the cruise ship weigh anchor that evening and disappear into the sunset. Don did not know it at the time, but he had just witnessed the beginning of what has now become an almost daily visit by cruise ships to this cove. What is now a six-hour out-island adventure for thousands of tourists has wiped a pristine little harbor for small boaters right off the map. He should have been used to this; hadn't the same thing occurred in many parts of Florida? How far did a person have to go to escape these incursions? Don decided to let the naturalists and the environmentalists ponder the problem. He had already calculated that he could stay ahead of this sprawl by virtue of his lifestyle. He just needed to keep it lean, mean, and mobile.

One day later than promised, the new starter motor arrived, and by the next day, there were only two boats in the harbor. On the evening before the Cigarette departed, a low flying aircraft flew over the cove. It skimmed the top of *Yutaka's* mast. You could see that it was a twin engine DC-3 even in the dark. The group sitting topside noticed a bright light shining a couple of miles offshore. Bill, the passenger on the Cigarette, thought that someone might be in trouble out there. He suggested that the guys take Don's boat and go to investigate. To Bill, Don said, "Sit down," because the last thing whoever was out there needed was help. Don said, "Bill, what you are seeing is a drug drop-off, and they sure aren't looking for company."

Matt and his crew on the "go fast boat," as Don's nephews referred to the Cigarette, were underway at the crack of dawn. It was a testament to the Islands, how eight adults of such dissimilar backgrounds could coexist in harmony for four days and nights, especially when you entered four kids into the equation.

Don remembered the story his brother had told him before they parted company the following day. He had been moved by this story that seemed to validate Ralph's early departure from the workplace.

Ralph recounted: "One day, the *Yutaka* was anchored in a small harbor in the northern Exumas. I happened to look over and see a couple on a small sailboat struggling to get their anchor secured. Thinking that they might need some help, not that I was a pro, I rowed over in the dinghy and volunteered my assistance. The lady on the boat, who appeared to be in her mid-sixties said, 'Oh, thank you, that would be so kind.' I put on my mask, dove to the bottom, which was not that deep, and secured the anchor by hand. When I surfaced, the lady thanked me profusely. She went on to tell me that she and her husband, who was her age, had always dreamed of sailing the Islands when they retired. They now realized that they had waited too long. The rigorous demands of sailing exceeded their diminished physical capacities. It was proving to be too much for them. Their lifelong dreams had been shattered, and I could feel their despair as I rowed back to the *Yutaka*."

Don knew that he had not waited too long, and he was glad that Ralph had not waited, either.

His brother was going back to the Abacos and then back to the States. As Ralph and family sailed north, he thought, maybe there is a god; certainly, a higher being was watching over them, and he hoped that being would keep his vigil.

Three months later, Pretty Patty stole two hundred dollars from Donnie and disappeared back into the drug-infested world that he had tried to rescue her from.

No matter, Don was creating his own dream, acting out his vision of life. He was not sitting around waiting for things to happen. He made some mistakes, just as others do in the march forward.

⌐ CHAPTER SIX ⌐

"Home is where the heart is."

UNKNOWN

BEFORE DON ACQUIRED THE *Oar Dog* IN 1978, he had found refuge in a variety of abodes. His itinerant lifestyle did not lend itself to a fixed spot for placing his pillow. Actually, Don had a little trouble finding a pillow that he could stuff into his cooler. Nine years as a vagabond wandering the Islands had brought him to the conclusion that he needed a fixed base of operations.

Real estate doctrine emphasizes the importance of a neighborhood. If you want to protect your investment, be sure and choose the best neighborhood you can afford. Don may not have been aware of this doctrine, but he, intuitively, knew what constituted a good location for him. He had been scouting the Islands for nine years. He was not as interested in protecting his investment as he was in locating the action. Action, in this case, meant three things: diving, women, and commerce.

West End seemed to meet all the criteria. It was a favored port of entry for those making the crossing from the States bound for the Abacos. It was also a convenient weekend stomping ground for power boaters. If the weather was good, they could zip over in a couple of hours and avail themselves of the diving, fishing, and nightlife.

The Jack Tar was the only resort located at this western tip of Grand Bahama Island. For those who have read Herman Wouk's *Don't Stop the Carnival,* the similarity between the Jack Tar and the hotel in that novel was

59

striking. A major construction project had produced a beautiful physical facility on a magnificent site. The problem was that there were just not enough trained locals to operate and maintain the complex. The Bahamian government mandated that local citizens be given the bulk of the jobs. This idea was noble in theory, but the end result was that everybody lost their jobs when the resort shut down after only a few years of operation.

When Don made his decision to set up a more permanent operating base, he chose West End. The Jack Tar was open then. The fact that there was only one resort was deemed to be an advantage. Unlike locations with multiple hotels and facilities, the people who visited West End had only one place to congregate. No bar hopping for the socially minded crowd meant that Donnie could choose his stool and wait. Sooner or later, some chiquita would take an interest in the tanned, muscular, hippie looking guy with the engaging smile. Further conversation would not diminish the impression that drew ladies to him in the first place. His only shortcoming, when first meeting him, was that he was short. Short in stature, but not short in other attributes. Tall women were quickly willing to overlook his height; however, Donnie, for his part, preferred women who were shorter than he was, at least for an extended relationship.

Once it was determined that West End would be his hailing port, he started looking for a houseboat. His search took him to Tampa, where he located a forty-five-foot, steel-hulled, Sea Going model. The engines on the boat were inoperative, but he was not looking for transportation; he was looking for a home. With the help of two friends, one of which owned a thirty-five-foot Trojan, they towed the houseboat from Tampa to West Palm Beach via the Gulf Intracoastal Waterway, the Okeechobee Waterway, and the Intracoastal Waterway. The total distance for the trip was just over three hundred miles, and it took place on protected waters. The remaining fifty-six miles required dealing with the Atlantic and the tricky Gulf Stream, which flowed north relentlessly but somewhat more passively in the summer. The winds from the northern quadrant turned that invisible river into one of Mother Nature's more formidable adversaries.

60

Oar Dog

While the group waited in Riviera Beach for a perfect weather forecast, they stocked the houseboat with provisions. Houseboats were not built with trips across ocean waters in mind. It was important to pick your weather correctly, and this task was made more difficult because of the slow speed at which they would be traveling. They guessed right, and with the exception of a localized thunderstorm that presented some temporary difficulties, the two-ship armada arrived safely at West End. There was much fanfare from the locals, as Donnie was a favorite at the marina.

The *Oar Dog* had made it unscathed. He wasn't thrilled with the boat's name, but Don shared the superstition of many boaters, that it was bad luck to change a vessel's name. He would make it work.

After backing the boat in and fussing with the lines for a while, Donnie placed his lawn lounge chair at the stern of the boat. He then mixed himself a cocktail and, for the first time, sat down and assumed the position that was to become his trademark in the Islands.

His lounge chair, or "throne," as he referred to it, was in easy reach of a secondhand TV dinner tray. Most trays of that type never made it to the secondhand state. Don did not have an interior decorator (at least as best as he could remember), and he had selected the tray, as well as the chair, because they were made of aluminum, and they would not rust in this nautical environment. The tray was necessary to hold his ever-present drink and the current book that he was reading.

His mission of setting up a home base had now been accomplished. He had his wraparound waterfront lot. He had location. Donnie was ready to hold court.

YOU MIGHT ASK, how could someone with such limited means afford a houseboat and the expense of towing it to the Islands? The lobster business couldn't have been that prosperous.

Don remembered how his ancestral blood had served him in good stead. He was twenty-five percent Scottish, twenty-five percent English, and fifty percent Irish by birth. There was just enough frugality in his genetic blueprint to allow him to save part of his earnings over the years.

When he recognized the need for more stability in his life, Don was still a little short, monetarily, of being able to make it happen.

Don had chosen a different path as a young man. Now, some ten years later, he was facing some of the same economic quandaries that his peers, who had chosen a more traditional lifestyle, were confronting. It seemed that even a nomad needed a roof over his head sooner or later.

Don had solved the other basic requirement in life by utilizing the sea as a source of food. He was able to trade the excess bounty from the sea for the other food items that he required.

Up until then, the barter system had fallen short of fulfilling his capability to provide a roof over his head. Donnie would not be lured down the conventional road in his quest for shelter. That would represent a sellout of his values, and that was too expensive a price to pay.

Instead, he chose to give the barter system one more try. The difference this time was the ante was higher. He would trade his knowledge of the water and boating for the cash that could be obtained for transporting merchandise that was heavily sought after, stateside. This was another fifty percent of his gene pool clicking in, the Irish side. Hadn't other respectable Irish families, such as the Kennedy's, been involved in the importation of illegal contraband? True or not, the stories that circulated, regarding how Joseph Kennedy amassed a fortune during prohibition by helping to satisfy the demand for bootleg alcohol, provided the salve that Don's conscience needed to get him into the import business.

He determined, early, to never let his role in the smuggling business expand. He would make just the necessary number of runs to get that roof for his pillow. It did not need to be a fancy roof either.

His fifteen-foot river skiff was all he had to ferry small loads of illicit cargo. With a limited capacity and an exposed storage area, his trips would have to be furtive. It was imperative that the trips take place under the cover of darkness. The risks were enormous. There were, of course, the physical risks, but the greatest threat in Don's mind was the possible loss of his freedom, if he were apprehended.

There were, certainly, others involved in the transportation of hemp, but what differentiated Don from most of them was his intellect and his determination to preserve a lifestyle of minimal trappings and maximum freedom.

Here, the remaining twenty-five percent of his gene pool kicked in. It was the English heritage that led him to resolutely persevere with his new undertaking (to persevere through the four trips needed to bankroll his search for a home). He drove his skiff across the Gulf Stream like most people drive their cars to work (at least those on the night shift). Just as most workers who have put in a good day's work, he was not the least bit ashamed of collecting his paycheck.

As soon as he had augmented his savings and stashed some money to live on, he retired and began the search that led to the purchase of the *Oar Dog*. His retirement came less than a year after he had entered his chosen career. There was more money to be made, but that was not Don's style. He was not into accumulation. Don was still young, and he did not burden himself with thoughts of retirement nest eggs.

FRIENDS COULD NOW LEAVE DONNIE MESSAGES. He was able to receive guests and to host small parties. He could prepare meals on a real stove, and most of all, he now owned a refrigerator. His quest for ice was over. Many boaters in the Islands spend an inordinate amount of time searching for ice, not to mention a substantial amount of money when they do find it.

Donnie needed ice for two dissimilar reasons. Firstly, his diving necessitated that he keep the fish or lobster on ice, and secondly, his drinking required a fair amount of cubes for his Cuba libras and his screwdrivers. Rum was his alcohol of preference for many years, until vodka entered the picture.

Ice cubes were an integral ingredient of any boat drink. Don loved to watch landlubbers struggle with a drink while a boat was skimming across the water. Typically, they would end up wearing the drink. The secret to mixing a boat drink was to use plenty of ice. It worked miracles.

Since he did not care for lobster, and since most men can't live on fish alone, Don's new refrigerator allowed him to store meat. He readily acquired this meat from the luxury yachts that stopped at West End. The folks on these floating palaces were usually anxious to trade for fresh fish; since, man cannot live on meat alone.

Much to his chagrin, Don felt himself growing accustomed to his creature comforts. West End may have been a small pond, but Don enjoyed an almost icon status of being the major amphibian or should that be fish in residence. The size of the pond would swell with the arrival of migratory boaters and tourists that landed daily on charter jets from all over the world. The one thing that these temporary visitors had in common was the pursuit of pleasure. People came here to have a good time, not to drop out.

With the *Oar Dog* parked in the middle of all this, Donnie became the ex officio Master of Ceremonies. The whole scene could be likened to a game show. The contestants were there to have fun, and Donnie was there to select the winners. The prize was an insight into the Islands that most visitors never saw. With the Master of Ceremonies acting as the guide, the finalists would be escorted to beaches and reefs that only a few locals had knowledge of. The scenario was the same one that Don would use over and over again. Let nature's beauty take its course. The major amphibian would just tread water waiting for the flies (or perhaps ladybugs would be more accurate) to come to him.

At this stage in his life, Don did not have an ounce of body fat. It seemed that no matter how much he ate or drank in the evening, his physical activity during the day (and the night, also) was more than sufficient to balance with his caloric intake. Any excess calories that tried to invade his body were met by a machine that thrived on exertion and was fueled by the oxidation of those little varmints that cause so much grief to the general populace.

COULD YOU BLAME HIM FOR GETTING COMFORTABLE with this lifestyle? Well, there were those who did. Two general groups tried to dissuade him from the niche in life that he had found: reformer friends and women, who wanted to make him part of their personal niche.

The reformer friends came in two varieties.

The first group knew of his intellectual gifts, and they felt he could make a contribution to society. In addition, they felt he was wasting his innate talents, and that these talents could bring him financial rewards. Don found that to be hypocritical.

The second group, former hell-raising friends of his, had been "born again." They had seen the "light" and joined the church. Obviously, Donnie was not a joiner, unless it was a party. He believed in the idea of a god; however, he was not into organized religion. It was his opinion that the church just served as a pulpit for various mortals like himself to interpret the teachings of God. It was the mortals who needed an audience, not God. Wasn't God omnipresent?

Don felt the teachings of the bible weren't that complex. Keep your hands off your fellow man and your fellow man's woman, and live together in peace and cooperation with your neighbors. Be kind. Help those neighbors when they need it, and personally ask for directions from above, when in doubt.

Being the son of a backwoods Baptist father and a Catholic mother, he had been raised in a fairly diverse religious manner. He and his brother were required to attend either church or Sunday school each week. The choice was up to them, except on Easter or Christmas, when mandatory attendance at Catholic Mass was required. As they got older, the choice tended to be influenced by whatever girl they were dating at the time.

A psychologist might have seen Don's view of religion in a different light, especially if Don had confided in him about two particularly traumatic days in church.

The first took place when he was nine years old and living in Denver. He and his brother had to spend a Sunday at his Aunt's house, because their mother and dad were both working. The brothers knew this meant that they would have to attend Catholic Church with her and their Uncle.

Walking to and attending mass with Mae and Malcolm was not something they were looking forward to. So they had hatched a plan. The plan was that they would wear blue jeans to their aunt and uncle's house. Since their relatives normally dressed up for church, as did everyone else in Denver at that time, they would probably get to stay back at their apartment until Mass was over. Wrong!! They had underestimated their aunt's resolve. This was an opportunity for the devout Catholic to influence her young nephews, and she wasn't going to let a chance to expose them to the church in which she felt they belonged pass. Both Don and Ralph were humiliated when they attended church that Sunday wearing jeans. The walk to and from church could be equated to the Bataan Death March of World War II. The participants were forever scarred.

The second incident, although somewhat lighter in nature, took place some years later, when Don was a junior in high school. He was attending a Methodist service with his main squeeze at the time. In their haste to hold communion and get to the collection, one of the deacons pulled the tray away from Don before he had totally removed the shot glass of grape juice. The result was a white shirt that resisted all future attempts to remove the purple stains. Ultimately, the shirt got tossed, but the stain on Don's brain was still there. Religious ceremonies would never be the same.

What always seemed to turn out the same was his role as Master of Ceremonies. Only the participants were different. Variety in this case was not the spice of life. The diversity was actually removing flavor, not adding to it. Don was confronted with the proverbial Catch-22. In an effort to maintain his vagabond lifestyle, he did not allow relationships to clutter his life with personal baggage; but the countless one-night stands no longer quenched his thirst.

Donnie needed to redefine the parameters that dictated his relationships with the fairer sex.

He needed to undertake a vision quest, but he was one of those rare Americans that had no Indian blood. It appeared to him that everyone he met was a descendent of one American Indian tribe or another. It seemed to be cool. If you had this native blood, then you must possess a high level of spirituality. Without this blood, was Don excluded from undertaking a vision quest? Not in his mind. Didn't the ancient Celts live close to the earth? Weren't they in harmony with nature? Yes, they undertook vision quests. The Roman Empire, the Feudal Era, the Industrial Revolution, and the Information Age have altered, but not erased, the genetic link with the past. For that matter, all people have evolved from a period when they were closer to the earth. Most people just don't bother to connect with those links; at least, that's how Don felt.

How could a person, who had purposely not gone to work for the last nine years, be uptight? He remembered something his brother had told him one day after he had concluded his voyage and rejoined the workplace. Ralph had postulated: "Man seems to seek a certain level of aggravation." In short, he meant that when you remove the big things in life that bother you, you tend to replace them with smaller things. Things that didn't bother you so much before now become significant sources of aggravation. It seems people need to have something to worry about. Maybe it keeps them from getting too complacent.

As Don sat naked on an uninhabited little cay, he was deep in meditation. This was not meditating as learned from a class or a book. It was just

67

instinctive contemplation. Maybe there was some American Indian blood in the closet. Donnie mulled over his sources of aggravation. He didn't like supermarket lines unless there was a pretty lady in line next to him. He didn't like entangled coat hangers in his closet. It annoyed him when someone slipped him a Canadian quarter in his change. There had to be something at a deeper level.

Ah! He had it, women. His relationships with women, while physically satisfying, had been vexing at best. Could it be possible that he had been at fault in earlier failed attempts to take an affair to the next level? Sitting on this cay with no name and no bar (he had left his cooler on the *Oar Dog*), he determined that he might just have to give up a tiny portion of his freedom in order to get to the next plateau in a relationship. Once he had satisfied himself that a small sacrifice on his part might be in order, it seemed to be a no-brainer. He would not have been here in the first place if he had achieved total Nirvana. This whole vision quest had lasted about three hours, somewhat shorter than the three and four day ordeals of the American Indians. If Donnie hurried, he could be back in West End in time for cocktail hour. He would be able to immediately put his new theory in action. Don forgot to put his Speedo back on until he took his little skiff off plane at the entrance to the harbor. The weight on his shoulders had been lifted. He had lightened up.

⌐ CHAPTER SEVEN ⌐

When the full moon's soft light
slides silver fingers o'er the sea,
and warm breezes caress gently
the Oar Dog at Treasure Cay.

Ahh, the beauty is so tender.
Draws to my eyes a tear.
While nature's in full blossom,
we know Donnie's in full gear!

BRUCE AND HIS GREEN APPLE
(A DEDICATION ON A BOOK GIVEN AS A GIFT TO DON)

THE NEWS THAT THE JACK TAR WAS CLOSING STRUCK HIM HARD. The disappointment that gripped Don drew out emotions that had never come to the surface before. It was not just the fact that the resort was shutting down or significantly scaling back. What really shook him was how comfortable he had become there. Slowly but assiduously he was becoming a creature of habit. Many of his friends had become creatures of habit and he had chided them for it. Now their guru was guilty of abandoning his freewheeling untethered way of life. His refusal to accept routine as a way of life was the hallmark of his identity. Don conceded that some routine must serve a hidden or biological need since most people seem to lapse into it, but if routine was just a mask for comfort then he preferred to wear his face in plain view. He had experienced his share of highs and had mucked through a few lows, and he would deal with this comfort issue later. The Jack Tar was closing, and he sensed that this was inevitable since they always had more employees than guests, even when they were at full occupancy. The marina would remain open for the time being, but everything was up in the air.

Once he had absorbed the news and thought about the options, Don shifted into his positive mode. He didn't have it so bad; what about all the people who depended on this resort to put food on the table, a roof over their heads, and support their families? This was just going to cut into his social life, not decimate the very fabric of his existence. He regretted his self-pity.

It was time to put plan B into effect. After mulling over several new potential sites for relocating his home, he concluded that the resort at Treasure Cay offered the most potential. Investors had sunk a lot of money into the property, including the marina, which was first class. The beach there was as pretty as any in the Islands. Don was sure, based on preliminary conversations with other boaters, that Treasure Cay would become the new destination of choice.

Towing the *Oar Dog* over the seventy miles of water between West End and Treasure Cay was not a major issue until you reached the last few miles. The majority of the trip was across a shallow bank with waters averaging about six feet, but the last few miles required a detour around Whale Rock. Don, with his ability to read the water, would have normally taken a shortcut through a shallow channel if he had been piloting his skiff, but the *Oar Dog* and the boat that was towing it couldn't make it. With settled weather, the passage around Whale Rock turned out to be uneventful.

Moving to a higher-class neighborhood meant that Captain Don was once again confronted with the issue of money. It would require a lot of fish and lobsters to pay the rent. Complicating matters was the fact that the best reefs were not as close as they were in West End. This meant he might have to hunt for square groupers again. Square grouper was the nautical

70

term for a bail of marijuana. Trade in this commodity had been ongoing, but Don had not been a participant since his acquisition of the *Oar Dog*.

Things would have to be different this time. He needed a larger and faster boat. A larger boat would minimize the number of trips that he would have to make, and it would also allow him to better conceal his cargo. A faster boat was not for outracing the authorities. It was necessary in order to minimize the time spent crossing the Gulf Stream.

Bigger boats were expensive and since Don was a cash basis citizen, he had no credit. His last purchase on credit was over ten years ago and that was his MG, which had been repossessed by the Bank of America. Well, maybe his brother could help him. He would, of course, not tell him the real reason that he needed a bigger boat. Don was not anxious to approach Ralph on this subject, but he needed to move fast, as contacts had informed him that a freighter was due in the Islands within a couple of weeks, and it needed to have its cargo transshipped promptly. As it turned out, Ralph was glad to help him, and he did so by cosigning a loan at his bank. He never even asked why he needed a bigger boat. Didn't all men need bigger toys as they grew older?

Three trips later, Don was retired again. He had made enough to cover all the boat payments and he set that money aside in separate coffee cans. His marina rental and estimated near-term living expenses had been covered too. Only his rent had gone up. The rest of Don's lifestyle continued to lack ostentation.

A Beach Near Treasure Cay

71

Once settled in at his new wraparound waterfront lot, he realized that the closing of the Jack Tar must have happened for a reason. His new surroundings revitalized him. There were new reefs to explore, there were new sights to take in, and there were new opportunities to avail himself of. He had a new boat and life was good.

THE SMALL AIRPORT AT MARSH HARBOR was improved, and soon the tourists began the flow into what had been a sleepy little Out Island resort.

The Swiss girls were gone, but he knew the next plane that swooped down on Big Abaco Island would certainly count among its passengers a French or a Scandinavian or a British lady seeking to experience an unforgettable vacation. It sure wouldn't hurt his feelings if just a good old American girl showed up. They were still his favorites.

As it turned out, a special American lady didn't show up, but Donnie did meet one on a trip back to the States. Her name was Tonia, and she had coal black hair that crowned a pretty head chocked full of brains that, in turn, rested on a gorgeous body. She had just moved to Florida from upstate New York.

Don was still sweating from a recently completed tennis match on the courts that abutted the sands of Riviera Beach. He was getting ready to join his *compadres* at the Beer Barrel, but first he needed to jump under the shower. He was in a line of one waiting his turn, and he had just wiped the sweat from his eyes when who should he behold but one of the most beautiful girls that he had yet encountered. She had her head down and her eyes closed to protect her from the torrent of water gushing from the shower as she tried to wash the sand from her short dark hair. Don could only watch in awe. When Tonia turned the shower off and opened her eyes, she saw Donnie, standing there staring at her. He was not leering at her (she hated that); it was a genuine look of admiration with no lust implied. She met his gaze, momentarily, and then let her own eyes inspect the inspector. They both felt a simultaneous exchange of cosmic energy as they stood there mesmerized.

72

He was the first to speak after what seemed an eternity. Despite all his previous experience with meeting women, the only thing that he could utter was a simple, "Hello!" However, he was able to back it up with a body language that spoke volumes. Tonia's reply was an even simpler, "Hi!" but her eyes said so much more.

These two simple words launched their relationship with more than sufficient power to break the barrier that terminates most human encounters from the start.

They stood there talking for at least twenty minutes in the heat of the sun. Don didn't want to blow this one, but he decided that a quick litmus test would reveal more about Tonia than a day's worth of conversation. He invited her for a drink at the Beer Barrel under the guise of escaping the sun's burning rays. This test would reveal how she would respond to his circle of friends who were far from ordinary, at least the ones that were in attendance at that time of the day.

Tonia opted for iced tea and, in a highly unusual move, Donnie asked Annie, the barmaid, to leave the vodka out of his cranberry juice. He was going to handle today's verbal discourse straight. He did not want alcohol to fog this encounter even if it went no further than an iced tea. They had not even finished their first drink, and Don realized that it was he who was being consumed. Every word that she spoke seemed to further distance her from the pack. She appeared so comfortable in this hangout that was a second home to him. Her presence brightened the otherwise dimly lit little tavern, but the glow that emanated from her was muted enough to make it easy on the eyes, and Donnie's eyes were not missing a thing.

Don had experienced lust at first sight several times, but this was a different, more expansive feeling. He remembered the day on that deserted little island and his mini-vision quest. Suddenly, the thought of sacrificing a small part of his freedom in order to make a relationship work did not seem like too steep a price to pay if it would help get this new acquaintance into his life on a more regular basis. All of this after less than two hours of being together. Why, he had not even slept with her, nor had she given him any indication that this might take place. He was willing to take his chances on his ability to move this budding liaison to that point. The real test would be going beyond the sexual aspect. How could he sustain moments similar to what he was feeling now—rapture? This was similar to what he had experienced in an oxygen-depleted state while diving. The big difference here was that he was sober in the middle of the afternoon, and his raptress was sitting across the table from him.

Donnie leapt head first into the relationship attached only by an emotional bungee cord. He was willing to stretch for this lady's affections.

Tonia, on the other side of the table, was surprised at how she was attracted to this guy so suddenly. She could almost feel the life force that Don exuded, despite the fact that a table separated them, and the table was not sitting in one of those romantic places that you see in the travel magazines.

The conversation flowed effortlessly, and the topics had substance, but the beauty was, their voices moved at a rate that allowed for thought to take place simultaneously on another plane. The rhythm of the words allowed for instant contemplation, thus rendering the responses and the counter-responses more meaningful. Isn't good conversation like good music? It appeals to senses that are normally blunted by the day-to-day cacophony that blasts the auditory nerves.

Tonia hoped there would be more of these conversations, and knew that she would entertain further overtures, should they be forthcoming.

Neither Don nor Tonia wanted this to be a "wham, bam, thank you, ma'am" type of affair, but that evening as they lay in bed, there was no lack of respect felt by either party. Forces not typical of one-night stands had drawn them to each other. The nature of the attraction didn't merit playing silly, coy games. They wanted each other, and they both knew it. Both were confident enough in their own attributes not to be threatened by the speed at which their lives had collided. They could deal with the fallout. The next two weeks further substantiated the initial impressions.

Tonia was smart and she was athletic. She had a sense of humor and a good personality, but unlike a potential blind date, there was no concern about her pulchritude. Tonia was by no means a lap dog, but she was obedient to the rules of Don's boat. Her standing naked at the bow of the boat may not have made the boat go any faster, but it sure did get the captain's heart beating faster. She embraced all of Donnie's aquatic activities with great fervor. She could hold her own in backgammon and scrabble. And surprise of surprises, she could play cribbage.

Don's grandfather had taught him and his brother to play cribbage when they were five and seven respectively. A game developed by lumberjacks to while away the night hours in the logging camps, it had followed the loggers across the northern states as they systematically decimated the original growth forests in order to supply the demand of an expanding country.

AFTER A TWO-WEEK STAY IN THE STATES, which was seven days longer than originally planned, Don headed back to Treasure Cay. It was always good to get back to the *Oar Dog*, and he had two fifteen-pound-plus bull dolphins (not to be confused with a porpoise) in the fish well. These were not particularly large by fishing standards, but they would yield some nice fillets. He would often throw a line over the side while transiting the Gulf Stream, more for sport than for a source of food. He still relied on his diving to put fish on the table. Don usually threw back whatever he was lucky enough to catch while fishing with a hook and line. Dolphins were the one exception, although he rarely kept these if they were less than ten pounds.

Throwing his cooler onto the *Oar Dog*, he thought to himself how nice it would be if Tonia were here to share this homecoming. The old houseboat was now his home. It had crossed the imaginary line that differentiates a shelter from a home shortly after he had purchased it some five years ago. But since only six lines had to be cast off in order to get underway, he still felt that his nomadic lifestyle was intact. The biggest threats to his way of life now were the recurring images of Tonia that swirled in his mind. What was the deal? Why did he, so badly, want to convert those images to reality? It was simple. He was smitten.

Don felt no value in just possessing things. He watched as old friends dedicated their lives to accumulation, becoming slaves to their style of living.

Certainly, people needed to attain a level of comfort, but how much comfort and security do you need at the price of the prime years of your life. That is the time when you are most able to physically and mentally participate in life (a time to explore those areas of interest that always seem to lurk just out of reach for most people).

"If I only had more time." How often had he heard his friends as well as others say this? He thought the answer was fairly simple. You must constantly monitor your comfort level to ensure that what you are doing, and how you are doing it, is really worth the cost measured in time. It is not the dollars you spend; it is the time spent accumulating that is the true cost. He was surprised at what a small price people seemed to assign to time.

The young, especially, seemed to squander it recklessly. Losing his friend, Butch, early had taught him how valuable time was. Others had suffered similar losses, yet they seemed to ignore or suppress the message. He was willing to concede, however, that having a family raised special issues, and he had difficulty making his philosophy on time fit into this particular arena. It seemed to him, on the surface, that monitoring comfort levels should apply to families as well.

Sitting on his lawn chair sipping a drink, there on the deck of the *Oar Dog*, Don decided that he put a high value on his time, and Tonia's full attention on a more permanent basis was something worth possessing. It was not Don's problem what other folks did with their lives.

As he walked down the dock in search of a pay phone to call Tonia, the word "possession" slipped back into his thoughts. Were many marriages or relationships doomed to failure because one or both of the parties were treating the other as a possession? In the rush to possess, did people fail to make the distinction between human and material collectibles? To a certain degree, maybe it *was* Don's problem what other people did with their lives (since no man is an island). Picking up the phone to dial her, he decided that borrowing Tonia might be his best strategy.

Tonia was thrilled with the prospect of visiting Treasure Cay. Donnie had painted such an alluring picture of his stomping grounds during the fortnight that they had been, constantly, together. She had been totally swept away by his charm and his vigor. His energy level, his enthusiasm, and his zest to fill his day with activity were balanced by a mind that seemed to be contemplating or assessing a bigger picture. She might have been reaching to describe him as a renaissance man, unless one viewed his lifestyle as an art form.

Like many other new arrivals to south Florida, she had been going through an adjustment period. A couple of jobs that did not work out had led to one that showed promise. She was working as a receptionist at a busy doctor's office. While answering phones and making appointments was not what she aspired to, it did put her in the health care business. Tonia really wanted to become a nurse. She had dreamed of doing this since she was eight years old, but her family's economic status kept nursing school from being an immediate reality. If she was going to become a nurse, she was going to have to be patient first. She was going to have to answer telephone calls before she could answer the calls of the sick. Tonia wished to administer healing, not to schedule appointments.

So how should she RSVP Don's invitation? To leave for the Islands would be a major interruption in the flow of her life; however, if she passed on this opportunity, she might be defining her life's path by default. What the hell? She was young, Donnie was attractive, the sick would have to wait. It was one excited and somewhat nervous lady who deplaned from the small twin engine Cessna that had just landed at Marsh Harbor Airport (or would airstrip be more appropriate). The air was warm and humid. An afternoon sea breeze held the sun's true heat at bay.

This was her first trip to the Bahamas, and her view from the low flying Cessna was spectacular. The tanned, longhaired, bearded guy waiting for her seemed to fit perfectly into the picture that was still being painted by her psyche. It was a mural that could have been created by Gauguin in his South Pacific studio.

The taxi, a vintage model Cadillac, driven by one of Donnie's local friends, whisked them away at about twenty-five miles per hour to the marina at Treasure Cay. She was anxious to see her new castle. The *Oar Dog* did have what might be called a moat around it, but the water that surrounded it was there to attract invaders, not to repel them. The *Oar Dog* was not a sterile looking mega-yacht. It was a sun faded, maturing houseboat that exuded ambiance. "Island Deco" was how Donnie described it as he threw Tonia over his shoulder. He did not cross thresholds in the conventional manner. An old window shaking air conditioner provided the sea breeze to the inner sanctum of this flat-bottomed barge of a home. The condensing water dripped from the air conditioner as it tried to handle the cooling load generated by the reunited couple. A flat-bottomed boat keeps a better secret of its owner's activities than a deep V hull, which tends to reflect the side-to-side movement of its occupants.

Don With Tonia on the Oar Dog

The last rays of the sun, which was rapidly retreating below the horizon, greeted Donnie and Tonia as they emerged from their floating abode. With the possible exception of *Gone With the Wind*, most matinees did not last that long. Unlike traditional Mexican siestas, a siesta in the Islands with Don could leave you more drained than rested, but it was a nice way to drain off any excess emotional energy.

Marching is the typical cadence of a parade, and based on the stares from other boaters at the marina, Donnie and Tonia were on parade. But strolling is the typical cadence on a dock, and that is how they proceeded to the open bar, located near the pool.

The seeds, planted during those first two weeks in the States, blossomed here at this remote little island paradise. Both knew that they had made the right decision. There was a little catch, though. Life in the tropics is subject to rapidly forming thunderstorms, storms that form in the troposphere on hot muggy afternoons, storms that produce violent squall lines from otherwise vapid, moisture soaked air. Thunder and lightning replace the sound of squawking gulls and the light of the sun. The dark gray clouds and the distant thunder signal trouble for lovers as well as boaters. For Donnie and Tonia, this was the *morning* of their relationship and it was too early for storm clouds to be brooding on the horizon.

When Don sat on his throne and held court now, he had a queen sitting on his lap (a real queen for those who would read something else into this).

Tonia was fun loving and extroverted enough to handle her role as co-master of ceremonies quite well. Her presence attracted females that might not have felt comfortable alone with Don. Couples replaced single female visitors, but the rules of the boat did not change. Married couples, who would have never thought of going naked in mixed company, now frolicked with reckless abandon as they explored reefs and deserted little islands. Couples cruising on small sailboats, couples cruising on big luxury yachts, couples flying in on private jets, and couples flying in on charter tours—the class distinctions disappeared when the clothes came off. Nudity revealed people for who they were, and it was surprising to many experiencing this for the first time just how natural it really was.

Don, of course, tried to push the bubble a little. He would stir the pot in order to move a boatload of naked couples into some sexual exploration. This did not usually lead anywhere because most pairs were content with revealing their bodies, but were not comfortable with sharing their mates; however, occasionally, if the chemistry was right, Don's Robalo would become the scene of a bacchanalian orgy.

Seeing others confront and work through sexual taboos brought Donnie perverse pleasure. He knew the participants would have to deal with some heavy emotional issues the next morning.

HIS SOMEWHAT JADED SEXUAL BEHAVIOR was not apparent to the native islanders whom he provided with fresh fish and lobster. Over time, he had befriended many of the locals who worked in the hotel and around the docks.

Local Friends

He would take Tonia with him on diving trips solely dedicated to supplying these friends with seafood. Often he would take specific orders for their favorite fish. Many of these locals were just interested in the fish heads, which they incorporated into delicious stews. In return, Don was often rewarded with a loaf of fresh, warm bread or some other home-baked pastry.

He was also affable with the younger Bahamians. Don would go out of his way to advise and encourage teenagers to make the most of their talents. He did not use himself as a role model. Teaching the smaller kids to fish with a casting rod brought him satisfaction. The younger boys and girls tended to be in awe of this slightly gruff and bearded denizen of the docks. The kids would build up their courage to approach him, but once over that hurdle, their rewards were bits of wisdom delivered at a level that they could readily assimilate. Stories frequently found their way back to the schoolyards and/or back to their homes.

Donnie spent a lot of time teaching the older teenagers to play volleyball. He loved the game; so coaching these naturally gifted athletes served three purposes. First, it gave the older kids an outlet for their talents. Secondly, it put their idle time to good use while building pride. Lastly, it made it easier for Don to put together a game, and he loved to play. He continued the tradition that was started when Don was living in West End. It was

80

a tradition of financial support. He used a portion of his earnings from the sea to subsidize trips for both the girls' and the boys' teams to travel around the Islands and even to the States for various competitions. The only stipulation was that the teams practice hard perfecting their skills. He had no use for athletes that squandered their talents due to laziness.

The dollars used to provide this support had a high cost. Earning that money had put his freedom at risk, as it came from his illegal ferrying service.

⁓ CHAPTER EIGHT ⁓

"Imports seem to overwhelm us today.
The dollars go out; we need them to stay.
Drugs are a source of this negative flow,
So think about that, while you study the glow,
And take heart in the fact as the embers subside,
Local growers are trying to stem the tide."

AUTHOR

A NEW ROOMMATE AND A DESIRE TO KEEP TONIA AROUND meant that Don was going to have to ratchet up his income a notch. In his eyes, he only had one place to turn. Jobs were scarce in paradise. As best as he could recall, there were no bosses or time clocks in Eden. However, there was a woman, and his woman would not want for the necessities, especially since her needs seemed reasonable. Tonia seemed to be in tune with his ideas as they related to comfort levels. She had a low threshold of comfort, and she did not require pampering.

When Don approached his connections in the import business, he sensed a change. Just as farmers often change their crops to respond to the demands of the marketplace, there was a shift going on in his line of business. While there was still a demand for ganja, another product had entered the marketplace. Cocaine was becoming the narcotic of choice for many recreational drug users. This created a whole new set of problems for the Good Old Boy network. The highly addictive nature and its influence

83

on a person's behavior was different than what these traders had been dealing with. Most chose not to involve themselves in the cocaine trade.

There were other factors at play. The Colombians, who were in control of the supply of the now fashionable drug, played by different rules than the loose knit Good Old Boy network did. The South Americans were highly organized and centralized. A lot of dollars were involved, and they played hardball. They had already developed a reputation for ruthlessness. The Colombians carried automatic weapons. The Good Old Boys usually carried none.

Worse yet, efforts to interdict shipments of this habit-forming drug were stepped up. This put real pressure on the importers of hemp. They were trying to get a bulky product past prying eyes, whereas a small amount of cocaine had the same market value as a boatload of pot.

Don resisted the urge to make big bucks by involving himself with the Colombians. Instead, he made two more, now riskier than ever trips for some friends, who needed to move some product, which was normally inhaled, not ingested, unless consumed in brownies or honey slides.

On his second run, he really earned his money. Over the years, the level of sophistication displayed by Don and others had increased. When he knew the timing of his run, Don would call a fishing buddy in Riviera Beach. The buddy would conveniently arrange to be fishing from the jetty that bounded the inlet. In his tackle box, there would be a handheld VHF radio. At the sign of any suspicious activity by law enforcement officials, he would contact Don using a coded conversation based on fishing conditions. The Robalo would have to be close to shore before contact was established, but nonetheless, it was better than no warning at all.

This particular night, as he approached the coast, his buddy warned him that a drug enforcement boat, disguised as a fishing boat, was sitting just inside the inlet. Don reversed his course immediately and headed north along the coast. This maneuver did not go unnoticed by the DEA boat, but the agents lost a few minutes getting their anchor in. They had a faster boat; however, the heavy seas mitigated part of this advantage.

As usual, Don had chosen his weather carefully. The trade-off for a turbulent crossing was the protection that rough seas provided in situations just like this. With the agents in pursuit, at a speed far less than their boat was capable of in calmer waters, both boats headed up the coast.

The darkness and the heavy seas made it difficult for them to see the Robalo, which, needless to say, did not have its running lights on. They expected their quarry would probably try to enter more tranquil waters at either the St. Lucie or the Fort Pierce inlets. Their guess was Fort Pierce since it was the safer inlet in these kinds of conditions.

They radioed ahead to request assistance at both inlets. Both the hunter and the hunted were taking a real beating from rapidly escalating waves born of gale force winds out of the northeast. Mother Nature was playing the role of a witch, busily stirring up her caldron.

This was a situation that Don had always dreaded. He had to rely on both his Robalo and the two Mercury engines that powered it not to let him down. The boat was pounding into the waves that were coming from his starboard bow. A speck on the ocean, it surged up over the waves at an angle and then down into the troughs in a sequence that repeated itself, one countless wave after another. He maximized his speed to the ultimate limit that both boat and body could endure.

Don knew that he did not have enough fuel to head back to the Islands, and even if he did, it would be daylight in a couple of hours, and search planes would certainly spot him, well before he could find sanctuary there. Warning lights went off in his mind: expect a welcoming committee if you try to reach either the St. Lucie or the Fort Pierce inlets. He hoped his pursuers would discount any possibility of his trying to go through the Jupiter Inlet under these conditions. It was the closest inlet, but it would be virtually impassable at night under these circumstances. Don knew this was his best alternative.

What the hell? If he ran aground on one of the constantly shifting shoals, he could kiss his boat goodbye and try swimming ashore. He didn't like his odds, and not being a gambler, this made it worse, yet. Adventure was the name of the game, and his adrenaline was pumping.

Entering this inlet was going to require focusing all of his knowledge of the sea into a few critical minutes. Still about one-half mile offshore, he continued just past the mouth of the inlet. He then swung his boat slightly over ninety degrees to port. The plan was to surf in until he was right in front of the cut. At that point, assuming he got there, he would come a few degrees to starboard, and gun his engines to negotiate the narrow channel marking the entrance.

With about 150 yards to go, his heart stopped as he felt the boat brush the bottom. Salvation appeared in the form of a wave that lifted him over the bar before he could run aground. Now inside the inlet, he afforded himself the luxury of a backwards glance. He was greatly relieved to see the flashing lights of his hunter's boat as it rose on the waves, still heading north toward the St. Lucie Inlet.

Don was thankful. Luck had been with him, and he doubted that, even if they had seen him, the agents would have braved the inlet on this particular night. His salt encrusted eyes now tried to focus on the lights shining from the shore that bordered the Intracoastal. He could not rule out a possible reception by the authorities. Apparently, they were concentrated further north. Don knew that it would not take more than another two hours before the officials concluded he had either turned out to sea or come in the Jupiter Inlet. They would be searching for him.

A trip up the Loxahatchee River seemed to be the best choice for evading detection. He wondered if Ponce de Leon had felt this much excitement when he became the first non-Indian to enter this inlet in 1513, and named the river La Cruz.

A hastily conceived plan entailed tying up behind a friend's house while he retrieved his boat trailer, which was attached to Don's old Bronco. There was a boat ramp nearby, and if his cargo, which was now covered by a tarp, went unnoticed, he would have it out of the water in a few hours.

His buddy was not aware of what lay concealed beneath the tarp as he drove Don to his mother's house some ten miles away. Don, normally, left his old Bronco and the trailer alongside her house when he was in the islands.

He thanked his friend, said "hi!" to his mom, reconnected his battery, and hustled back to retrieve the boat, which was sitting unattended with only a thin tarp protecting a cargo worth thousands of dollars. The Good Old Boys might not be so good if this cargo fell into someone else's hands.

Even though the boat ramp that Don planned to use was out of the way and usually not that busy, he waited until about 9:00 A.M. to pull his boat. There was always a lull in the action around boat ramps at that hour. The fishing mavens had long since launched their boats, and the recreational boaters were still eating breakfast, if they were even up.

As in all skills relating to boats, Don was proficient in extricating his vessel from the water. Watching neophyte skippers confront the frequent travails associated with getting their craft safely back onto its trailer could be an amusing way to spend a Sunday afternoon.

With his yellow boat still dripping water, Don headed back to his mom's wondering whether the good guys, who were looking for him, had stopped for coffee and doughnuts.

He wasn't out of the woods yet. His cargo was now sitting in the middle of a busy residential neighborhood. The consignee of the goods would have to provide an alternate point of delivery. On all of his previous trips, the cargo was delivered to a house on the water. After a lot of scrambling by the consignee, Don was directed to an old Quonset hut located on some ranch property west of town. His familiarity with the local streets, allowed him to take a circuitous route, thus minimizing his time on the busy thoroughfares that crisscrossed the south Florida landscape.

The whole process was getting burdensome, and he was anxious to get it behind him. He thought there must be an easier way to make a few bucks, but no new inspirations came rushing to mind.

As his trailer plied the final six miles of dirt roads, he had to slow down in order to keep his cargo from bouncing right out of the boat. He was loaded right up to the gunwales. Don was being granted an insight into the next stage of distribution, and this made him wary. The knowledge of where the bales were broken-down into one-pound bags could become a liability. On the other hand, his employers were extending a signal of trust. Still, he preferred to remain on the edge of this shadowy business.

He was very much opposed to the legalization of pot. It would put him out of a job. He did think it was out of character for the government to pass up a chance to tax and control a substance that a certain segment of the population would smoke anyway. The more successful the Feds were in curtailing the supply, the higher the price went. You could deal with the social issues and use the taxes to fund a substance abuse program, and there would still be money left over. Most importantly, the government could then focus on the drugs that posed a real threat, such as cocaine, heroin, or a host of chemically created, mind-altering substances.

His boat now empty, but still in tow, Don headed off to go shopping. He always took advantage of these trips to the States for stocking up on food and parts for the boat, and there was a perpetual list of items that his Bahamian friends needed. He stopped by a sporting goods store to pick up some baseball equipment for a team that he was sponsoring. The team was comprised of fifteen and sixteen-year-old boys, and the financial support that he provided helped assuage any guilty feelings generated from his involvement in an illegal enterprise.

The next stop was a jewelry store. He wanted to buy Tonia a pair of earrings. A little surprise for the lady who brought him so much pleasure.

Prior to launching his fully loaded boat, he had one more stop to make before putting to sea, a short visit with Mom. She had promised to make him her special egg salad sandwiches. No unusual ingredients, there was just a lot of love that went into their preparation. She got high marks for presentation too. She would cut the sandwiches into four squares after squeezing the finely chopped eggs and mayonnaise between two fresh and soft white pieces of bread. Then she served them stacked in a high pyramid on a small plate, which magnified the quantity available for consumption. Donnie did not worry about his cholesterol intake as he attacked the pile. A straight Pepsi helped wash down these almost bite-size sandwiches, which had a tendency to stick to your gums.

On a Visit to His Mom

He thanked his mother, kissed her, and handed her four hundred dollars. The lunch didn't cost that much, but a round trip ticket to Boston, for a visit with her sister, did.

With the inlet behind him and calm seas ahead, Don set a course for Walker's Cay. It was a point of entry. He would skip West End on this trip, since it made for a longer passage back to Treasure Cay. The next night Tonia was wearing her new earrings when they tumbled out of bed in the midst of a passionate display of affection.

～ CHAPTER NINE ～

"Life is a train of moods like a string of beads, and as we pass through them they prove to be many-colored lenses which paint the world their own hue, and each shows only what lies in its focus. From the mountain you see the mountain. We animate what we can, and we see only what we animate. Nature and books belong to the eyes that see them. It depends on the mood of the man whether he shall see the sunset or the fine poem."

FROM EMERSON'S *Essay on Experience*

DON STILL HAD A DEMON THAT NEEDED EXORCIZING. It seemed that as soon as he let a woman into his life, a smoldering compulsion to abuse would begin bubbling just below the surface. The abuse would explode to the surface when he perceived any challenge to his authority or his masculinity, and these two traits were tightly interwoven. His expectations of a woman's role in life were almost pre-Neolithic. On the other side of the coin, before the abuse boiled to the surface, he was very kind and even protective. Once vented, his abusive nature would quickly sink out of sight. In his younger years, the catalyst was always alcohol. His companions never knew when he would cross the line. One minute he would be happy-go-lucky, and in the next minute, he would be in a rage.

All the women who cared for him, except his ex-wife Rachel, endured this abuse for a time in the hope that they could help Don. It was as if Rachel and Don had reached an early accord. He did not want the

91

Don Relaxed and Under Control

mother of his child exposed to a behavior pattern that he himself had just become aware of. Perhaps too, he did not want his daughter to have to grow up in an abusive environment. In any case, it was not long, despite his love for Tonia, before she met the Black Fairy, his demon with wings. She was willing to excuse the first incident as an accident brought on by alcoholic over-indulgence, but the second time that Don struck her could not be ignored. Despite her strong feelings for him, she packed her bags and flew back to the States.

This was a crushing blow to Don. Sober, he understood and respected her decision. How could he have let her slip away? Why couldn't he control this Black Fairy that didn't even exist in his rational mind? He knew alcohol was the culprit, but alcohol also brought him pleasure. After several years of spending January as a teetotaler, Don had dismissed the exercise as unnecessary. After all, hadn't all those dry Januaries proved that he was not addicted to booze?

IT WAS AGAINST THIS BACKDROP that something more sinister than alcohol came into his life. One day, while sitting on the deck of the *Oar Dog* and still brooding, two young Bahamians approached him with a package in their hands. The two boys played on one of the teams that Donnie sponsored, and the package that they carried was hidden in a first basemen's glove. The boys seemed to know what the white powdery substance in the zip loc bag was, and they were anxious to get rid of it. They told Donnie that they had found it floating along the beach about a mile away, but the boys were afraid to turn it over to either the authorities or their parents. The two asked Donnie if he would turn it in for them. Don agreed, and praised the boys for their course

92

of action. Maybe, some of the dollars he had earned from his smuggling activity had been wisely spent, sponsoring teams for the local kids.

Don was now in possession of a decent-size bag of pure, very valuable, cocaine. He had steered clear of this drug up until then, even though he had seen many others snort their noses full of the powder. As Don stashed the bag below, he was already wondering if it might be worth trying, or should he just sell it? No sense giving it to the authorities. They would probably sell it or use it themselves.

Had this incident occurred at another time in his life, the outcome might have been different. Donnie was psychologically vulnerable to the lure of this highly addictive substance. He was on the wagon in the hopes that a sober Don would be able to get Tonia back into his life. For five days the package remained unopened.

His friends were aware that Don's uncharacteristic behavior was the result of Tonia's departure. They gave him space while he was sorting things out.

Curiosity, temptation, and moroseness combined to ignite the urge to experiment with the cocaine. Mixing some of the white granules with some baking soda and chopping the mixture with a razor blade, as he had witnessed others doing, he created a thin line of dust about two inches long. Taking a straw, Don placed one end in his nostril and the other end over the line of powder, and snorted half of the dust. Switching nostrils, he snorted the rest of it. The rush that followed launched Donnie into a period of his life that was marked by urgency and, ultimately, paranoia.

He did not need to mask the use of this drug in the same way that many of his working class buddies had. Don was free to snort to his mind's content. Availability was the only constraint, and, in the Islands, this did not prove to be much of an impediment.

The cocaine seemed to amplify what was already a free and easy lifestyle. Unfortunately, this was an illusion. In actuality, it began to dictate and define his life, but, of course, this was not obvious to him at the time. Don had always been a little hyper below the surface of his laid-back demeanor; now, he was hyper a lot.

Stoked up on cocaine, Don was a whirlwind of action. The problem was the period after he came down from the high. By the time the contents of the Ziploc bag were gone, Donnie was firmly hooked. Maybe it was even sooner, since as his supply ran out, he was already making plans to obtain some more. When he purchased his first gram on the open market, Don realized you did not have to be a financial genius to determine that this was going to be an expensive habit. Alcohol, in the quantity that Don consumed it, was not cheap; but the cost of a fifth a day paled in comparison with the expense of doing cocaine on a regular basis.

This new drug did cure Donnie's lovesickness, but like most medicine, it eased the pain and ignored the source of the malady.

In the beginning, Don's friends were glad to see him lifted from the malaise that had altered his fun loving lifestyle. Their delight was tempered when they saw the source of the cure. The friends who had witnessed the destructive impact cocaine had on others were concerned. Some of his friends already dabbled in the drug, and, unfortunately, some came under its influence by virtue of their association with him. He was generous and would share whatever supply he had with both old and new acquaintances. Lines that resembled military parade formations would cover the miniature parade ground that was hastily set up on the dining room table of the *Oar Dog*.

A heightened sexual experience was one of the pleasures derived from the use of this white powder. The benefit was soon offset by a knee-crushing low that invariably followed the consumption of this drug, which exhilarated on one hand and demobilized on the other. To recapture the high, you needed more cocaine. Don was smart enough to recognize that this pattern was, in fact, addiction, and he was addicted. He was caught up in the cycle.

Underwriting the cost of this habit through diving was out of the realm of reality. The memory of his last pot run was still vivid. It was getting too dangerous to slip this bulky cargo past the Feds. This whole thought process brought him to one unavoidable conclusion. Perhaps it was time to talk to the Colombians who had approached him earlier with respect to doing business.

The South Americans knew of Don's reputation. People did not prepare resumes in this line of work, but you could be sure that they did check references. Once they had made the necessary inquiries, an invitation was extended. Like all major corporations, they held an orientation for their new hires. The Colombians did not discuss retirement plans or group insurance. They discussed group assurance and the consequences that deviation from your job could have on attaining the retirement years.

This little seminar was held on Norman's Cay in the Exumas. This cay was just south of Saddle Cay where he had done his stint as a caretaker a few years back. Things had changed since his last visit to the island. The first thing he noticed, as he pulled his Robalo up to the dock at the base of the hill that distinguished this cay from some of its counterparts, were the armed men who helped you tie up your boat. These same men discouraged any pleasure boats from either tying up or anchoring in the adjacent waters. In the pre-cocaine days, it was not unusual for a family cruising on a sailboat to be anchored next to a trawler loaded with pot. If everyone minded his or her business, it was live and let live. This was not the case now that the drug cartels were involved.

Nothing that Don had seen so far did anything to change his preconceived ideas of what working for these people would be like. In fact, he was very uncomfortable with the whole scene. A person attuned to minimizing comfort levels is especially affected when you start chipping away at the few that are left, and Don was a victim of this phenomenon. Up until now, he worked as an independent contractor. The Colombians wanted to exercise more control. They worked more to a schedule, without consideration of the weather and other factors—very much similar to the U.S. Postal Service. Don, on the other hand, preferred to use the weather and other factors, such as holidays or weekends, when planning his crossings.

His logic seemed to fall on deaf ears. The cartel was paying the big bucks, and Don had already calculated that it would take about four trips to set him up for a few years. The trade-off was acceptable under those circumstances.

95

Crossing the Gulf Stream in good weather afforded Don a chance to contemplate, as usual. He never fished, while traveling west with a cargo, until he was within ten miles of the coastline. Fishing was used as a cover only when Don deemed it appropriate. The sight of a sheriff's vessel made it appropriate. The sight of a gray, Marine Patrol boat made it inappropriate. Why risk a fishing license check, or an inquiry regarding the size of your catch, when you were carrying a cargo for which there was no license?

His thoughts that day dwelled on escalation. The whole cocaine thing was propelling his life forward at a rate that was jeopardizing his fun loving, free flowing lifestyle. He had been sucked in—hook, line, and sinker. Not only was he using this vacuous powder, he was making it available to others by virtue of his smuggling. This seemed to be a violation of his no harm, no foul doctrine.

It was his third trip. The money was good, as promised, but collecting it at the completion of both of his previous trips had provided him with two tense experiences. The lower echelon flunkies, who handled the payroll function, were always armed with automatic weapons. Worse yet, the payoffs had taken place off of Hole In the Wall, which was a small anchorage at the southern tip of the Abacos, normally a very deserted place, except for cruising sailors, who used it as a jumping-off point for Eluthera, Nassau, or the Berry Islands.

Part of Don's payoff came in the form of the very cargo he was transporting. This payment certainly fit the definition of a fringe benefit.

After his second trip, he carried an olive branch to Tonia who had found an apartment at the base of the bridge linking Singer Island with Riviera Beach. Located on the southeastern corner of the bridge, it provided a great view of the procession of boats that traveled in and out of the inlet, as well as a view of the sunsets across the Intracoastal Waterway.

His olive branch was in the form of a beautiful and expensive gold necklace. She loved the gesture, but she was not sure that she cared for Don's new level of existence. With the gift had come a promise, the promise was that he would only touch to caress, not to clobber. He kept his promise, and

96

their relationship was rekindled. Donnie made a conscious effort to reduce his consumption of cocaine, and being with Tonia made it easier.

Tonia felt more comfortable with the home field advantage, and Donnie did not make an issue out of her not returning to Treasure Cay. He had money in the ground, and he figured with two more runs things should be pretty well positioned for the future.

Approaching the coastline on this, his third trip, Don was pondering the wisdom of his employer. He was concerned that the Colombians always wanted their goods delivered to the Miami area. On his first trip the delivery point was behind a home situated just north of the Haulover Inlet on a small island where Al Capone had once resided just a few doors away. His second trip had terminated further south behind a residence located on Starr Island. This home had overlooked the cruise ship terminal that was located about a half-mile to the south.

These were waters that Don was not familiar with. This added to the tension that was always there, no matter how many trips he had made. The Haulover Inlet was one of those exits from the sea that was very susceptible to the weather. It could get quite nasty; however, on the night that Don had transited, the sea conditions were tolerable. The Inlet at the Port of Miami was one of the better ones that dotted the coast of Florida. The problem here was the amount of commercial boat traffic that took place at all hours of the day and night. In addition, there was a Coast Guard base located just off of the main channel into the harbor. Don had opted to take the longer way around Key Biscayne, and he then doubled back through Biscayne Bay to reach Starr Island.

As he negotiated lumpy seas on this, his third trip, he was concerned with the location of tonight's destination. His drop-off point was behind a home located on the Coral Gables Waterway. This meant he would have to negotiate a narrow, unfamiliar channel, which had been created with hundreds of pounds of dynamite and that led right underneath busy U.S. Highway 1.

Following a course similar to the one used on his second trip, he rounded the lighthouse at the end of Key Biscayne and entered Biscayne

Bay. Proceeding past the ghost-like structures of several houses built on stilts and located far offshore, he pointed his boat toward the maze of lights that dotted the shoreline of the bay to the west. He had to rely on his charts. Don had never traveled by boat on the waters that abutted the shoreline of this part of the bay. He had to pick out a green light that flashed at four-second intervals from the myriad of white, red, and green lights that filled his eyes. These were eyes that had been failing him since his days at the Naval Academy.

He mused over how his future might have turned out had he remained at the academy. Would he have had command of a destroyer by now? Would he have the benefit of young eyes, provided by the lookouts on the bridge when he approached an unfamiliar harbor? Would he have a sharp young lieutenant to do the navigating? Idle speculation, he needed to clear his brain of these thoughts. Reminiscing was a recurring event on all of his crossings. It provided an escape from the reality of the stress created by the business he had gravitated to. Try as he might, he could never quite rationalize, to his own satisfaction, that what he did was proper. Well, he had no lookouts and no navigator, so Don was going to have to rely on his own tired eyes and his own instincts to get him safely into port.

The bay was calm as he sped across it on a bearing that his charts indicated would get him to the mouth of the waterway. About a mile offshore, Don slowed to a speed that left no wake. There were several shallow spots and if he ran aground, Don wanted to do so at a slow speed.

His helmsmanship had been perfect. He spotted the flashing green light just slightly to port, but what he also spotted sent alarms going off in his head. There appeared to be a boat coming out of the very waterway that was his destination. Don had been traveling without running lights. Should he switch them on now? If the approaching boat was a pleasure boater, he might brand Don as just another ignorant boater, but it was unlikely that a pleasure boater would be out at three o'clock in the morning.

The most likely scenario was that this was a vessel operated by the sheriff's patrol. Don's heart palpitated, but his mind was clear and focused. If he turned his lights on and it was the sheriff, then he would draw immediate suspicion. Without his lights on, he was going to draw their attention too. The option of turning and running was not viable. The Robalo could easily be run down by the speedy boats that the Dade County Sheriff's department used. Donnie would have to rely on a glib tongue to bail him out of this jam. Fortunately, his cargo was concealed, and it would only be detected if the deputy boarded and searched his boat. He had to keep him off of the Robalo by allaying his suspicions.

It was only moments after he had determined this course of action that he was blinded by a searchlight in his face. A voice soon followed over a hailer requesting that he put his engines in neutral so that the speaker could come alongside. The voice also told him to keep his hands where they could be seen. Coming alongside, the deputy asked Don to tie a line to one of his starboard cleats. The deputy wanted to know why Don was out here at this hour, and why was he operating without running lights. Don told the deputy that he had left North Palm Beach earlier the previous day on his way to visit his sister-in-law. He had stopped to fish and was unable to get his boat restarted. He went on to say that it took him almost seven hours between the time he determined that a wiring problem was the cause of his trouble and the time that another boater had seen and responded to his distress signal. The Good Samaritan had helped him to get his engines jump-started. Don further related that turning off all of his equipment that ran off of the battery, including the lights, seemed to be the prudent course of action as he continued on his trip. Finally, he explained to the deputy that he had exercised great caution so as not to endanger other boaters.

The deputy, who was no kid (you usually had to have seniority in order to get the marine beat), looked at the salty, bearded, captain and shook his head knowingly. He had been involved with boats, himself, long enough to know that they could be prone to breakdown as a result of the hostile environment that they operated in, as well as the neglect of their owners. The deputy had two questions, though. "What was his sister-in-law's name, and where did she live?" Don responded, "Betty Kiley and she lives about

99

three quarters of a mile up the waterway." The deputy seemed satisfied with this answer, and he quickly shifted the conversation to small talk about the fishing further up the coast (if there is any such thing as small talk when conversing about fishing). It could be lonely patrolling the bay at night, especially on weeknights. After almost twenty minutes of chatter, Don handed Roger, now a friend of sorts, the line that had been holding the two boats together, and waved goodbye.

It was only then that he could sigh a deep breath of relief. Thank goodness that his brother had mentioned to him a couple of years ago that his sister-in-law, Betty, and her husband had purchased an older house on that waterway and restored it. Don had no idea where, exactly, it was.

Proceeding slowly up the canal, the pace of his heart was just now beginning to match the pace of his boat. He was looking for a dock displaying red and green lights in addition to the more functional white lights used by most people. The colored lights would distinguish his destination from the other docks that were attached to every house built here during the late forties and early fifties. Latins presently owned many of these homes, and it was an *hola* that greeted him as he slid up to the dock, which seemed to be still festooned in Christmas lights. No sooner was he secured to the dock cleats than the lights were replaced with darkness.

This point in an illicit crossing always made Don very nervous. He felt extremely vulnerable being secured to a dock with a boatload of contraband. There was both the consignee and the law enforcement officials to worry about. His major concern now was the Colombians. He had read too many books and heard too many stories. Don carried a .38 pistol, but this weapon would be hopelessly mismatched if things got to that. Besides, with his failing eyesight, he couldn't hit the broadside of a barn door. There was no small talk between him and the two *senors* who unloaded the powder. An hour later, Don pretty well exhausted his Spanish as he departed the dock with a hearty *buenas noches*.

Not only was his Spanish exhausted, but his whole being felt like it might be able to match Rip Van Winkle in a little contest. Instead, he settled for a three-hour nap, once he had reached the bay again and dropped his hook.

THERE WAS A FINE LINE between his dreams and reality as he clawed his way back to consciousness. These are the thoughts that fill a person's mind as they try to separate the dreams of their sleep from the contemplation of the day ahead. The period of limbo when you know that everything is okay for the moment, and you are safe with your thoughts, as long as you don't move. Alas, life does not often allow one to sustain that position for very long. It is up and at 'em. The military has a way of ending those moments abruptly with reveille. Civilians use an alarm clock to destroy the ambiance of those moments. On this day, the hot sun was the villain. Scorching rays of light interrupted his contemplation, but not before he had reached a major decision. Don would make no further trips for the South Americans. What he was doing was wrong, and he could no longer disguise it under the guise of putting a bottle of rum on the table.

How did one give notice that he no longer wished to work for a company when their employer is the drug cartel? He had never met his real boss. He had no address to send a letter of resignation. He normally received his instructions regarding the pickup and delivery of his cargo from a pretty blonde who would show up at the *Oar Dog* for a short visit. The Colombians had done their homework well. A pretty blonde visiting his old houseboat would certainly not be an unusual event. Still, Don did not want to tell some messenger that he was no longer interested. Something might get lost in the translation. He also had money due him from his last run. Don decided to face this problem head-on. After receiving his payment at Hole In the Wall, he would head south to Norman's Cay, but first he would drop off the money at a trusted friend's house in Nassau. Don could not help but think, when he heard the expression "a trusted friend," that this was redundant. Wasn't trust part of what separated friends from acquaintances? In his mind you were not a true friend if he couldn't trust you.

101

While en-route to collect his money, Donnie stopped at Little Harbor, which was a well-protected, but rather small anchorage on the eastern tip of Big Abaco Island. A brass foundry operated by a family of extraordinary artisans was located at this tiny dot on the map. The family had arrived there many years ago by schooner, and they comprised the total population of this remote spot. Don wanted to purchase a special statue for Tonia's coffee table, and everything these artists created was special. He described what he wanted, which was a pair of divers (one male and one female) descending over a shark. He was told it would take several weeks to complete a unique piece, which was fine with Don.

As he rounded the eastern most point, which provided what little protection the anchorage at Hole In the Wall afforded, he saw a sleek Donzi already at anchor. There was no doubt that this was the pay wagon. With some of his previous earnings, he had purchased an M-16 rifle. A couple of his friends who had served in Vietnam, suggested that he increase his firepower. They did not feel that a pistol was a sufficient enough weapon, given the expanse of the water and the armament of the people that he was doing business with. He had it readily accessible beneath a beach towel lying on the bench seat behind him. He just didn't trust these guys despite the fact that this was his third payday. There were three men visible on the Donzi. That was one more than usual, so this added to Don's already suspicious mind. This spot on the ocean was a very lonesome place, as are most spots on the sea. Don was on his own. One of the men waved, and as Don approached he could see that they were all smiling. "*Buenos dias!*" they hollered. Donnie replied, using the same words. "*Tenemos el dinero,*" they continued. "*Grande,*" Don responded, calling on his wealth of knowledge of the Spanish language, which consisted of two year's worth of high school courses that he had grudgingly taken as part of a college prep curriculum.

All he wanted to do was exhaust his grasp of conversational Spanish with a *muchas gracias* and a *sayonara*—or was it *hasta la vista?*—and be out of there. Coming alongside the Donzi, Don did not even offer a line;

instead he offered an outstretched arm. Just hand him his money, and he would be underway, no more gibberish was necessary. The Colombians understood the gesture of the outstretched hand, and they placed a canvas bank sack in it. Donnie nodded, and the other boat's occupants gave him a sly little smile as he idled right on past them. About twenty yards in front of their bow, Don gunned the engines and brought the Robalo up onto a plane. He never looked back, but he jerked his boat to starboard in the event that someone was sighting their rifle on his backside. When he was out of sight of the Donzi, Don altered his course for Nassau.

His stay in Nassau was brief. Dropping off his sack of money, now concealed in a duffel bag underneath some clothes, he headed for Norman's Cay. Giving his notice was going to be tough, but he was relying on some sense of honor on the part of the Colombians to understand his position. His choice of doing it at Norman's Cay seemed preferable to having them come snooping around Treasure Cay to find out why he had turned down an assignment, or consignment, whichever was most proper.

As an unexpected visitor, he was greeted with some concern. He asked to see Pablo, who was the person that he'd talked to on his first and only other visit to the island. His request was granted, and after a short wait, he found himself sitting on a verandah overlooking the Tongue of the Ocean, which was the name given to the deep water that protruded onto an otherwise shallow bank that made up this part of the Bahamas. The deeper water was a darker blue than the shallower water that covered the banks, which was almost lacking in color.

Pablo spoke the English of a very well educated Colombian. He asked what brought Don to the island. Don wasted no time in telling Pablo that crossing the Gulf Stream with illegal cargoes was getting old. He went on to say that he had been doing it long before meeting Pablo. The cargo may have changed, but the tension was the same. Donnie also told Pablo that his unfamiliarity with the waters around Miami made him vulnerable to detection. He then said, "Loose lips sink ships," a maxim that Don had picked up during his short stay at submarine school. Pablo could rely on

Don to keep his mouth shut. This educated director of illicit operations was aware that Don had done a very professional job of moving merchandise, and he felt that this bearded gringo could be trusted. This was not always the case with some of the other captains. He told Don that maybe he would change his mind in the future, and if he did so, they would be glad to avail themselves of his services. The last thing he said to Don before they parted was, "Señor Don, just remember the cartel has a saying too. 'Loose lips are dead lips.'"

It was a relieved and happy skipper who parted the docks at Norman's Cay that day. He visited in Nassau for a couple of days, and then headed with his treasure back to Treasure Cay. Enough—this was as close to working for a living as he wanted to get. There was too much pressure. He was going to revert to his former lifestyle.

⌒ CHAPTER TEN ⌒

TREASURE CAY
(Pronounced Key)

"When your troubles mount like a ton of bricks,
And you wish to escape and be free,
There's a place, my friend where your dreams come true
It's the Beach at Treasure Cay.

You'll love at once this land of ours;
You'll live real happily
When you give your heart to this fair spot,
To hold in custody.

So pack your bags and join us here:
Bright clouds and the bluest sea;
There's rest of body, peace of mind,
On the beach at Treasure Cay."

FROM C. H. LIGHTBOURN's *Poems With a Point*

THE INCESSANT DRONE OF THE *Oar Dog's* AIR CONDITIONER was in total harmony with Donnie's sleep pattern. What does a person dream about when he leads a life that so many yearn for in their moments of reverie?

105

Well, there were a few chinks in the armor. Three things bothered him and they were the stuff of nightmares.

The first was his occupation, or part-time job. The second was his attraction to the product that his job evolved around. The third was a problem that had been with him much longer than either of the aforementioned, and that was a predisposition towards spousal abuse. He expanded the conventional definition of spouse to include any woman who might spend more than one evening with him. In a normal state of mind, he was fully aware of how totally wrong and unnatural this behavior was. He never planned to strike a woman; it just happened.

Don was back on Treasure Cay and he awoke to a light but persistent tapping on his door. Since he slept with a pistol near him, anyone that knew Don would not enter his room while he was sleeping. He awoke with a last second promise to himself not to squander his time in paradise. The person tapping on his door was Mattie, one of the locals who worked in the dock office. She apologized for waking him, but Tonia had called, and Mattie thought that Don would want to know. "Damn straight!" and he thanked her profusely.

Tonia, now a nursing school student, had a ten-day break in her classes. Could she pay Donnie a visit? Silly question. Hop on the first plane, Don told her, and he would take care of the ticket.

The money he still had from his last trip combined with what he had already stashed away provided a nice cushion for the future. Don was going to have to revert back to his old style, and let his Scottish blood dictate his spending habits. The price for a free spending lifestyle was a price he no longer wanted to pay. No more moonless crossings.

The arrival of Tonia back on Treasure Cay was a source of relief for many of Don's friends. Maybe she would snap him back to the Don of old. Even though the two had reconciled back in the States, her return to the Island sent a strong signal. The skyline was soon infused with the brightly colored sails of Don's and Tonia's windsurfers. These pregnant surfboards with sails were an ideal means for exploring the shallow waters

106

that enveloped the areas around Treasure Cay. The boards granted them access to smaller islands, which held bigger boats at bay by virtue of the lack of depth of the water that surrounded them. Carrying a small cooler and a beach blanket, they had the makings for an instant picnic, a little lunch and a little hanky-panky. It was possible to sandwich in a little sexual horseplay. Since they sailed naked, they were not encumbered with the ritual of undressing for a bout of lovemaking. These were days that totally lacked tension, and this *joie de vivre* carried over to the evenings. Donnie was still doing a little cocaine, but more as an after dinner drink, not the mood altering, personality reinforcing cocktail or happy hour drinks, which many people used to make the transition from a hard day or week to an uncertain evening.

WHEN DONNIE PUT TONIA BACK ON THE PLANE for the States, he felt comfortable with his situation in life again. He resumed his diving, which had been placed on the back burner during the last several months. The frenzied pace of those months had been fed by the three midnight runs that he had undertaken and by his accelerated use of the white powder that he transported.

Several mornings, Don had awakened to the sight of blood on his pillow; and worse yet, on several occasions while submerged in the middle of a dive, he experienced difficulty swallowing. A few weeks later, blood began showing up on Kleenexes during the day as he attempted to clear his nose, which seemed to be constantly congested. You did not need to be a biofeedback guru to figure out that there was a cause and effect thing going on. Still, Don chose to ignore it. He would deal with it later. Things were going too well, and maybe this would be self-correcting.

Donnie's dance card was full. He and the *Oar Dog* were playing host to a succession of different visitors. Friends, whom he had invited to visit him over the years, all seemed to have chosen the next several months to take him up on his offer. These friends came alone, came in pairs, and even in groups of four. True to the adage that buddies can sometimes be your worst adversaries, the constant socializing inevitably led to some form of

107

brain alteration. Whether it was alcohol, weed, or cocaine; some mood enhancing substance always seemed to come into the picture.

The tenth set of visitors was a former cohort from his high school days and his wife. Jim had shared many interests with Donnie, mostly outdoor activities such as riding and camping. They had also shared dreams together in front of campfires as sixteen-year-olds. Jim was an intelligent, as well as an athletic, kid, and Donnie respected his views and opinions. Both Jim and his wife Beth, who had also known Donnie from those years, were appalled at the transformation that had taken place in their host. Others may have observed this, but Jim was the first person with the courage to risk Donnie's wrath by addressing the subject. "What are you doing to yourself?" he blurted. Jim could not hold in his feelings. "You are wasting away; you look drawn." Donnie, who had never been heavy, had noticed recently that his Speedos needed to be cinched up a bit more, and he also thought the face peering back from the mirror was a little more haggard than the one looking into the reflective glass. No one had said anything though. So he figured it must just be his imagination.

When Jim confronted him, Donnie did not take a defensive position. He listened intently as his friend scolded him in a fashion that only buddies could do to buddies. In a nutshell, Jim told Donnie he needed to get a grip on himself. Donnie could not help but realize that Jim was right. He was on a collision course with a steamroller, and that behemoth was going to crush him into a flat line on the road to hell.

Donnie reasoned that his quest for a laid-back lifestyle should not result in his becoming roadkill on the path less traveled. Cocaine, however, exerts a tremendous influence once a person falls under its spell. Despite his strong willpower and his abundance of intestinal fortitude, Donnie was losing the struggle with that white dust, which seemed to permeate every wisp of air that passed through his nostrils. Unlike the stench from his dad's stale beer, you couldn't just wash it down the sink. The fear was that the whirlpool created by washing away this drug would take him down the drain with it. He had become so dependent on cocaine that Donnie could not imagine life without it. His efforts to cut back were only temporarily successful. The periods between snorting the now shorter, thinner lines were consumed with the anticipation of the next self-allotted ration of nose candy, a feeling similar to what cigarette smokers who are trying to quit experience. Only, it is magnified by a more desperate sense of urgency.

THE YEAR WAS 1982, and Don's daughter, who now lived in Orlando, was turning sixteen. Don had decided to use some of his earnings to purchase Leigh a car. For the last eight years, she had usually spent at least a week or so during the summer visiting with her dad. Despite appearances to the contrary, he loved his daughter, and as she grew older, it was easier for him to relate. He made a special effort to be on his good behavior whenever she came to stay on the *Oar Dog*. Leigh, at sixteen years old, was already displaying some rebellious traits of her own. She had inherited a fair share of the genes that comprised her father's makeup. During previous visits with her dad, Leigh had seen him strike several women. Even though on his good behavior, Don had been unable to fully control his emotions. As a young teenager, Leigh had been verbally tongue-lashed by her dad, but he never struck her. The common thread was alcohol, and in the last two years, it was alcohol and cocaine that seemed to alter her dad's otherwise friendly personality.

With some money, which had literally sprung from the ground behind his mother's house, Don purchased for Leigh a small four-door Isuzu. He wanted this to be a special gift, and Don made an extra effort to buy ribbon with which he wrapped the car. The shiny new auto was presented with great fanfare.

Unfortunately, there was a big problem. The car was cursed, or at least that is how Leigh perceived it. Before she totaled it, which was less than a year later, the shiny little car, purchased with ill-gotten money, had been involved in more than one accident, and the driver had received more than one ticket. Perhaps the car was not cursed. Maybe it was Leigh's

Don and Leigh at Her Graduation from Auburn University

109

way of telling Don that she would rather have a Dad than a polished piece of machinery on wheels.

RETURNING TO TREASURE CAY, Donnie continued to expend his life force at an accelerated rate. His designation as a laid-back Out Islander was no longer applicable. He continued to pursue the same activities, but with diminishing enjoyment. One interest that did suffer was his reading. It was no longer possible for him to sit still long enough to concentrate. When he came down from his cocaine-induced highs, he would immediately slip into a deep sleep.

Don awoke one morning to a persistent voice calling: "On the *Oar Dog*! On the *Oar Dog*! Anyone Home?" Boating tradition forbids another from boarding your boat without first getting permission. Boaters often lean from the dock to pound on the hull in order to get the attention of someone down below. This persistent voice emanated from a Bahamian official in a white uniform, which substituted shorts for pants. Don exited the *Oar Dog* from the door located at the stern of his houseboat. Still groggy, he wiped the sleep from his eyes before balancing his specs on the bridge of his nose. Donnie was immediately aware that Constable Rolle was not wearing the smile that usually adorned his face. Inviting his unexpected guest aboard did not seem like a good idea, since there was no telling what might be lying around. Instead Don stepped up onto the dock. He was somewhat shorter than the Constable, so the conversation would not be done on an eye-to-eye basis. The gist of the conversation was that certain people had made innuendos that Don and some of his peers might be linked to the Colombians on Norman's Cay. The Bahamians had been monitoring boat traffic to and from that little island. Was this just a hunch on their part, Don wondered, or had they really seen his Robalo at Norman's Cay? His guess was that Constable Rolle was not here on the basis of rumors. "Sure, I've been there several times," Don replied. "When I am in the area, I always stop at the small marine store for fuel and ice. I have friends that used to care take the house on Saddle Cay, which lies just to the north. While

110

visiting with them, I discovered a lot of good diving spots, and I return to dive there as often as I can. The Colombians have pretty well taken over Norman's, and they sure don't make you feel very welcome."

Constable Rolle seemed to be satisfied with this response, but he cautioned Don about associating with the South Americans. Before departing, he told Don that he might have some additional questions in the future. As the Constable walked off of the dock, Donnie wondered how much the authorities really knew.

This brief conversation ended what had been a long period during which Don had been worry-free. He may have worried when in the act of moving the drugs, but once the goods had been delivered, Don had not given much thought to being discovered. Paranoia is a typical side effect of abusing cocaine, and now Don was concerned with something new lurking in the shadows. His life on this idyllic little corner of the world was self-destructing. It was time to seek both solace and help from Tonia. He was actually hesitant to intrude on her life, as she was studying hard for her nursing classes while working part-time as a waitress. He knew his brother would help. But Don was not anxious to reveal the extent of his slide into dependency on this albino dust that had dissolved his independent lifestyle in the same manner that the sands of time crumble even the mightiest monuments of civilization.

DON HAD GIVEN NO INDICATION of his impending visit. A knock at her door announced his arrival back in the States. When Tonia opened the door, she immediately sensed that something was wrong. "I need your help," was all that Don could say. Tonia grasped the significance of this simple request and delivered humbly, but with a trace of pride framing those four simple words. She had never heard him ask anyone for help and neither had anyone else. Her response was momentarily delayed as these thoughts went through her mind. "Yes! I love you. You know I'll help you."

This was going to be a major intrusion into her life, but she was studying to become a nurse so that she could help others. Here was someone she

111

loved. She certainly wasn't going to turn him away. Don realized the weeks ahead could be difficult. He told Tonia to quit her job as a waitress. Don would take care of her living expenses.

There was a problem though. Tonia's apartment was just around the corner from the Beer Barrel. While Tonia was at class, Donnie started visiting his old haunt. A couple of drinks with the guys, and soon Don was being exposed to the very nemeses that he was trying to escape. "Just a little," was how he responded to repeated offers to indulge in a line or two. He was trying to wean himself, but the temptations were great. The Beer Barrel was indeed haunted with too many memories of good times.

Tonia's patience and understanding were being put to the test. One evening after one of his matinee sessions at the Barrel, Tonia noted blood dripping from Donnie's nose. Despite his protests, she made him an appointment with a doctor for two days hence. She had a break from class, so she accompanied Donnie on his visit.

This hastily scheduled visit proved to be the turning point in Donnie's struggle with cocaine. Dr. Sherman asked Don if he had ever used cocaine, but he knew the answer before Don even replied. What the doctor saw was a mass destruction of the cilia that cleanse the breathing passages. Small talk during the visit had divulged that Don was a diver. What Dr. Sherman said next went right to the essence of a free diver. "You need to give up your diving. You are going to swallow one day while submerged, and that swallow will be your last act before you die." Donnie's body went suddenly numb. He wasn't afraid of dying, but he sure didn't want to give up his diving.

The doctor had struck a nerve that all the others, who were trying to help him, had missed. For a minute, Donnie sat there while his mind exploded with a burst of visions from his years of diving. Memories of positive experiences and pleasure overloaded his brain. It gave him a rush. He was high. What an idiot he had been to think that a cocaine-induced high could replace all the natural highs that he had experienced.

With this new awareness, Donnie was sure that his snorting days were behind him. The long silence that followed Dr. Sherman's warning was finally broken when Don got to his feet, hugged Tonia, and said, "Thanks Doctor. How much do I owe you?" Don knew that he owed the doctor a lot.

Leaving the office, he told Tonia that she would meet the real Don before too long. Donnie had made up his mind to give up drugs permanently, and to forego the use of alcohol for the immediate future. He was going to reclaim his life. Tonia had heard this all before, but her instincts told her that this time he was serious. She could endure the crap for those first three weeks or so if he made an honest effort. The year was 1983, and Donnie had just turned forty. It had been a tough year, but as a young man he would never have envisioned the difficulty blowing out the candles of his birthday cake would present. His lungs had borne part of the abuse that he had put his sinuses through. Tonia helped him blow out the remaining candles.

One month later, Don set off to Treasure Cay for his final exam. This would be the real test. No alcohol had crossed his lips and nothing but air had entered his nostrils for the last thirty days. Confidence exuded from the owner of the *Oar Dog* as he sat on his slightly tattered throne reading a book for the first time in many moons.

One by one his friends stopped by to pay him a visit. Amazement was the common conclusion that they all shared after talking with him. Out of respect for what Captain Don was trying to accomplish, they worked hard to keep temptation out of any activities. His true friends did this, but his so-called party friends were not that sensitive. Those acquaintances were soon putting lines in front of his face. Well, Don was having none of it, and when someone confronted him with nose candy, his response wasn't very sweet. No one tempted him twice. His wrath soon got the idea across that messing with his recovery was not a good idea. Several grams of powder ended up being flushed down the head rather than into someone's head. More than one mirror was smashed mixing glass particles with the crystal particles that had reflected from them before they were offered to Don. A few coffee tables bit the dust too. Don did not take kindly to those who sought to drag him back to the quagmire that he had just escaped.

The clear waters around Treasure Cay hardly resembled a swamp and

Donnie was soon exploring the reefs again. Years spent prying around the landscape that existed a few feet below the ocean's surface had made him comfortable in an element that most people might visit for a week or two every few years. The popularity of scuba diving had grown over the years, but Don was surprised at how much these organized dive trips missed. Once neophytes had been certified, their goal was to buy expensive equipment and to make deep dives. Don had done this in his youth, but over the years he realized that everything that he sought from the sea was within fifty feet of the surface. On an unpolluted reef, a kid with a snorkel could see as much splendor as an adult with two thousand dollars worth of diving gear.

AS PART OF HIS RECOVERY, Don had resolved to expose more of the local kids to this sub-surface paradise lying so close to their small island shacks. Volleyball and baseball were important, but these youngsters needed to realize that nature had bestowed a unique treasure on their islands, and this gem in the ocean needed to be preserved. When these young Bahamians matured, it would be imperative that they protect this haven from commercial exploitation.

The satisfaction that he derived from this endeavor was another example of a natural high that had been right under his nose. It was truly nose candy. The sweet memories that were created lasted into the future, unlike the temporary drug-induced rush, which was usually forgotten by the next morning.

Many of these economically disadvantaged children had never been on a boat the size of Don's Robalo, and that alone was a thrill, as they sped across the water. Donnie's little dive school soon added another subject. Rod and reel fishing was added to the curriculum. Scholarships to Don's "School of the Water" were available to any wide-eyed kid who showed an interest. A scholarship was truly a full ride for the lucky kids who took advantage of Don's generosity.

For three years Donnie bounced back and forth between the Islands and the States. He had won his battle with cocaine. Alcohol was still part of life, though, but even this problem had slackened.

114

The *Oar Dog* was still the center of activity on Treasure Cay. It was a slightly lower level of activity, as the participants were getting a little older.

For Don's working class friends, it was interesting to observe the parallels between Donnie and themselves. The year was 1986, and it was winding to a close. Many of his older buddies had placed Don on a pedestal. They had not expected his free and easy lifestyle to land him in a position not unlike their own. Now in their forties most of these guys had not been beaten down by their immersion in the system any more than Don had been by his disdain of that very same system.

This was a shocker, a tie, and an unexpected result in the game of life. Had Don's bout with cocaine altered the result, or was it the prolonged consumption of alcohol that had influenced the outcome? Was the outcome predestined? Was there a personality defect at work here? Donnie was not dumb. He had consistently scored in the top four percent, academically. He was street-smart as well. Now, as he sat on his deteriorating throne, the image of a burnout had replaced the image of a guy who had the system by the balls.

This did not bring any satisfaction to his buddies. It was not consoling that the hard way and the easy way led to the same place. It was much better to think that there were alternatives on the road of life.

What was not readily apparent was the hope that still resided within Don. His physical being had taken a beating, and his psyche was pitted from overindulgence, but he wasn't ready to throw in the towel. Working with the kids had given his life new meaning.

IT WAS A BITTER MAN WHO PACKED HIS THINGS onto an already overflowing Robalo early in 1987. Constable Rolle had been back. This time he'd been accompanied by an officer from the Department of Immigration. Don was informed that he had overstayed his welcome. It had been nineteen years since he'd first immersed his flippers in Bahamian waters. He considered the Islands to be his home. It was not so much that he had fled America, but he had found his niche in those waters. Don had come there a young man in search of adventure, and now he was leaving as a forty-four-year-

115

old, who'd made his mark, both good and bad, on this little watery dot on the map. This was indeed a midlife crisis. Funny how a midlife crisis strikes most men closer to the end of their lives than the middle.

Donnie knew why he was being asked to leave. Constable Rolle had taken him aside and told him that the government had some pretty solid evidence that he had been involved in smuggling contraband from the Bahamas to the United States. The good work that Donnie had done with the kids had not gone unnoticed. For this reason, he had been spared prosecution. Several of the kids that he had helped now held important government positions, and they had used their influence to have him deported rather than arrested. He would be allowed back into the country after six months, but only for limited visits and his stays would be closely monitored.

Over the years, Don had visited several other areas to check out the diving and the possibility of relocation in the event he ever had to leave the Bahamas. He was not blind to the possibility that his risky work might put him in jeopardy one day. He had ruled out Hawaii as being too expensive. The California waters were too cold. The language was a barrier in Costa Rica. It was expensive to fly to the islands further out in the Caribbean.

Don knew the *Oar Dog* was not up for the trip across the Gulf Stream, so with great sadness, he put it up for sale. Squeezing his most important possessions aboard the Robalo, and there were not many material items that had achieved the status of *important*, he couldn't help but cringe. Where had all these things come from? His mobile lifestyle had certainly been compromised. Shit, if he hadn't either given away or left so much on the *Oar Dog*, he would have needed a moving barge.

The locals had thrown a major bon voyage party for Donnie. Lots of tears and sad farewells, rum runners but no place to hide the sorrow that was painted on the face of those in attendance. Steel drums were beating in the background and mushy goodbyes were blurting in the foreground. Donnie had a hug and a smile for everyone. He had spent too many years developing a carefree image to let bitterness mark his last evening in the

Islands. A soft breeze and a moonlit night. This was the stuff of books and movies, a perfect script, a perfect novel, but for the very sad ending.

As he rounded the bend leaving the Marina, Don did not look back. He was not a sentimentalist, and he had closed the chapter on this part of his life.

⁓ CHAPTER ELEVEN ⁓

"Night falls, but it never lays down;
Reclining, it waits for the rising sun."
R.C. LEONARD

DAWN HAD NOT BROKEN WHEN HE CRANKED UP THE OLD BRONCO and drove south in search of a place to live. His destination was the Florida Keys. Donnie had spent the last two weeks at Tonia's apartment pulling himself together. When he came through the inlet, the mark that denoted the Robalo's water line had sunk some four inches below the surface. This was neither a safe nor a fuel-efficient way to head anywhere in his boat. He had hauled the boat and put it on his trailer, which now stood parked next to his mom's house.

Tonia had listened intently and compassionately as Don spilled out his disappointment at having been uprooted from his paradise. Surprisingly though, he was handling it pretty well. Paradise had been marred by his encounter with cocaine, and this disenchantment made losing it easier to deal with. The two of them sat together considering new courses of action. All the action did not take place at a cerebral level. Spontaneous horizontal activities interrupted the work of this two-person think tank. Alternatives were weighed. They cogitated and then recogitated.

It was an enigma that Don was a planner, but he was not a dreamer. He lived for the moment. The problem with living for the moment occurs when the moment ends. What are you going to do with the next moment?

119

Moments should be treated from the view of a going concern. There are no guarantees, but statistically, you are going to have a few more moments. Planning was an accommodation to this line of thought. It enabled Don to maximize his moments.

Don set the bottle aside. This was going to be a clear and rational determination. An easy choice emerged from this process. The Florida Keys were best able to assimilate a person with Donnie's background. There were a lot of stories similar to his own, which had found an ending at this last stop for so many dreamers and drifters who were just not content with traditional lifestyles. The endings here were not always pretty, but many square houses were filled with round citizens (citizens who had definitely been around). Donnie, with his Bohemian lifestyle and all his eccentricities, would fit right in. In fact, he thought he might seem quite normal to many of his neighbors.

The vote was unanimous (two to nothing). Both Don and Tonia agreed that the Keys were the place.

THE RUSTING, BLUE BRONCO was up for the task at the start of the trip, but it was gasping by the time it crossed the Seven Mile Bridge. Don coaxed it along until his search ended at Big Pine Key some twenty-six miles east of Key West. He had slowed down in compliance with the signs warning drivers to avoid smashing into the small key deer, which sought refuge amongst the mangroves and the Australian pines, or casuarinas, as they

120

were sometimes known. Driving at such a slow speed, Don was vulnerable too. Another sign caught his eye. "Happy Hour" had commenced at a little tavern. Even with his imperfect vision, he had spotted the sign as he crawled along that searing stretch of the Overseas Highway in his open Bronco. It was as if Mother Nature was compensating by enhancing his other senses.

The native Big Piners, who were in the process of supplementing their happiness, extended Don a hardy welcome. Over a couple of cocktails, Don was able to ascertain that some nice rentals were available. This surprised Don, since his first impression of the key was that it was nothing special.

Winding his way back through an artificial wall formed by a thick cluster of trailers, he discovered a treasure. The pirates who used to lurk in these waters did not leave this treasure. These channels of water had been created by some developers in a place where there had been none. Much to the chagrin of environmentalists, they had blown gouges out of the coral, which comprised part of the fragile ecosystem, in order to create waterfront lots. The damage had already been done. Don could not correct that. So he started his search for a suitable house. It did not take long to find a residence that struck his fancy. He paid his first year's rent in cash. Donnie did not want to have to worry about monthly payments.

His new borrowed home stood on pilings. The house was built that way to protect it from flooding. A hole had been blasted in the coral that supported the house. A slip had been built in the void created by the dynamite. This allowed Don to literally park his Robalo in the basement. The boat was sheltered from the sun when not in use, which was rarely. From his elevated abode, he commanded a view of a waterway that had been blown out of the coral also. He was only four houses from the open waters of the sea. Technically speaking, his canal opened into the Gulf of Mexico, but nature and man had combined to connect the Gulf and the Atlantic via an intricate web of channels. Markers placed by local boaters marked the maze of shallow channels.

Don didn't think the Bronco was quite ready for a return trip, so he caught a bus back to West Palm. The passenger manifest on a bus leaving

121

the Keys could be best equated to the Okies' westward migration in John Steinbeck's *The Grapes of Wrath*. The difference here was that instead of squeezing into dilapidated old trucks and cars, they all chose to take the bus. A few foreign tourists and some sailors on leave from the naval base in Key West brought some normalcy to the zoo.

THE ORIGINAL PLAN WAS TO PILOT the boat down to the Keys. Don would then return with the Bronco and fetch the empty trailer. He now realized that there was no way that his rusting old sports utility vehicle could handle the task.

Bill, one of Don's boating friends from the Beer Barrel, offered to pull the Robalo down to Big Pine Key in return for a place to crash on any of his future trips to the Keys. Don happily took Bill up on his offer. Oddly, it was Bill's boat, several years ago, which had towed the *Oar Dog* to its home in the Islands. Bill was a typical example of Donnie's network of buddies. Donnie had done a lot of favors over the years, and he never asked that they be returned.

In Bill's case, several years earlier, Don had swum a line from a yacht that he was a passenger on over to Bill's boat, which was floundering in a squall. The boats were in the middle of the Gulf Stream, and they could not get close enough to toss a line, so Don had jumped in dragging a light line, and braved the waves before nimbly timing his reach for the dive platform on Bill's bobbing boat. A cold dripping Donnie yanked himself aboard, shook Bill's hand, and said, "Looks like you could use some help?" They pulled a heavier line over and tied it to the bow. The yacht towed Bill's boat back to West Palm. Bill figured that he still owed Don a few favors. He was glad to be able to return one now.

LIFE ON BIG PINE KEY was working well. The neighbors were friendly and prone to partying. Living in a house rather than on a houseboat had its advantages. Size was the primary difference. A bigger kitchen provided more space for food preparation. Over the years, Don had developed into an excellent cook. People who dined with him for the first time were often surprised at his ability to serve a delicious meal. Meals by Chef Donnie were not fancy, but the food sure did appeal to the taste buds. Pangs of hunger were replaced with smiles of satisfaction.

The bedroom was bigger, and he had replaced his bed on the water with a waterbed. This new home for his pillow frequently resembled the Gulf Stream in a twenty-knot blow out of the north. The waterbed would surge and undulate in rhythm with the storm of passion taking place on the sheets that covered it.

A bigger living room allowed for more guests. On the *Oar Dog*, guests had to spill out on to the dock in order to avoid spilling their drinks on each other. There was plenty of room for both his broads and his boards (Tonia, Marilyn, and Susan and cribbage, scrabble, and backgammon).

The house was a modest, two-bedroom, one-bathroom nest perched on concrete stilts; but in comparison to where Don had been living over the last ten years, it was a palace built on marble columns. Donnie had changed kingdoms. He had a new place for his throne. It was on the balcony that overlooked the finger canal directly behind his perch.

Don had defied the old adage that you can't go back. He had metamorphosed in reverse. He had gone from a man in a midlife disaster back to a younger thinking man with great expectations. In the evolution of life, Don was a tadpole again. What pond would he choose this time?

There was a catch, though, an Achilles heel. His mind may have been given a second chance, but his body still wore the scars of abuse, and most of those scars were internal. Right below the surface lurked multiple skin cancers waiting to reveal themselves. Deeper, his liver and kidneys had suffered from constant abuse. Don had a strong heart, but it was pumping to some weakened organs. His revitalized mind was driving a jalopy that qualified for antique plates. Externally, the body was fit. Through all his travail, Donnie had taken care of the body that was visible to others. His aerobic system had been compromised, the cocaine had done irreversible damage, but Donnie at half speed was still ahead of most.

For Don the uniform of the day was still his Speedo. His walk-in closet was only 25% occupied, but the drawer that held his Speedos contained an assortment of faded colors. He did keep a couple of relatively new suits for special occasions. When he was just hanging out at his elevated little nest, there was no uniform at all. He literally hung out. If there were a knock at the door, he would wrap a towel around himself until he had determined the intent and nature of the visitor. It was back to nature if the visitor was a friend; otherwise, the towel sufficed. Don did not feel that clothes make the man. The one possible exception was a spiffy little Speedo. He was a card-carrying member of the Naturist Society. The problem was, where does a nudist carry his or her card? The real badge of membership was plain to see.

WHEN DON LIVED IN THE ISLANDS, he had returned to the States on more than one occasion to attend special events, especially volleyball tournaments held at nudist camps around the State. He had traveled as far as Pennsylvania to participate in tournaments sponsored by nudist organizations. Next to diving and sex, volleyball was his favorite physical activity, and nude volleyball gave him a chance to display his other talent as well. Nudist camps for the most part are very proper, family oriented places, but when Donnie and his friends arrived, they interjected a little spice. These were not finely honed athletes; however, they were folks who played hard during the day (an evening of naked revelry usually capped off a day of naked rivalry). Darkness ultimately clothed all the participants, as excess weight, wrinkles, and other scars faded into the black. It was as if the night provided clothing to the needy. Just as in crossing the Gulf Stream with a load of contraband, a moonless night was preferable to a moonlit night. There were some exceptions, but for the most part young, lithe, nubile bodies were not the rule.

Donnie was an older and wiser warrior now. He had become the Old Bull in the story of the Old Bull and the Young Bull. He was no longer in search mode. Instead, he grazed patiently waiting for a situation to develop, and it invariably did.

Tonia was still his main squeeze, but she resided 150 miles away, and she showed no inclination of narrowing the distance. Over time, she had determined that taking up permanent residence with him would be a one-way trip to disaster. She felt that their unique relationship would suffocate if both were confined in close proximity for an extended period. They both needed air, room to breathe. Don knew in his mind that Tonia was right, but his loins sent a different message. If he could clear the aching in his loins, then the pain of being apart would dissipate. So he would. He would cure the aching with whoever might wander into his pasture. Thus, Don and Tonia's relationship remained intact, intense, yet intermittent.

NEW WATERS MEANT NEW REEFS, and new reefs meant a new source for fish and lobsters. Don was soon exploring. He brought his knowledge to bear in an effort to find spots that hadn't been picked over by the competition. Unlike the Bahamas, the Keys were readily accessible by car and by boat and by cars pulling boats. Popular reefs were very patriotic places. Awash in dive flags, divers had to be cautious when surfacing, lest they bump their heads on the virtual armada of small boats anchored above. In some spots the state and the Park Service had installed permanent moorings. This was an effort to curtail the damage being done to the reefs by the anchors of those bobbing armadas of fiberglass.

There was a lot of water around the Keys, and the further you went into this chain of islands the more dispersed the divers were. Key West, itself, was an exception, as it was a destination point for hordes of vacationers. Don concentrated his diving on small, out of the way reefs. The reefs here were not as pretty as those in the Bahamas, and he was interested in reliable spots for finding fat, lazy groupers, or pretty pinkish hogfish, or maybe some decent size snappers. Over the years, his senses had overloaded on the beauty that surrounded living coral formations built on the foundations of their dead predecessors.

Commercial lobstermen saturated the ledges with their traps. These were hardworking guys, so Donnie always avoided areas where he saw their Styrofoam buoys. The lobster men may have had the advantage of generations of knowledge as to trap placement, but Don knew a lot about

125

where lobsters liked to reside, and he was willing to go to them in their element, not wait for them to come to him as the commercial trappers did.

Most of Donnie's neighbors plied the waters in one way or another. Many fished and/or dove. Others just cruised on their boats, availing themselves of the calming effects of the water and the beauty of the sunsets.

Donnie was quickly accepted in this neighborhood where "live and let live" was the generally accepted rule. A person's past was not an appropriate topic of conversation. Past life regression in the Keys often referred to the life or lives an individual had experienced before moving to this chain of islands that ended so abruptly in Key West. Although Don enjoyed his privacy, he could hit the switch marked *extrovert*, and immediately turn on a personality that drew others into his life. Many reclusive residents of Big Pine Key were drawn out of their cocoons by his charm and the frank, down-to-earth way that it was delivered. Donnie knew that he had inherited this trait from his dad, and he was grateful for a positive gene to offset the curse of alcohol that had been part of that same inheritance.

His diving skills soon became apparent to those who lived in close proximity. They would see Don cleaning lobster and fish on a regular basis. This intrepid diver could usually find a reef located on a lee shore, so weather rarely prevented him from diving. A bad hangover was more of a detriment than brisk winds, and just as winds slowly but surely develop into gales under the proper conditions, Donnie's drinking habit began to justify the posting of storm warnings. He had never stopped drinking, but he had cut back during the period that marked his departure from one set of islands to the latest set.

Don was a victim of his outgoing personality. His gift of gab was requested at the ongoing cocktail hours held by neighbors. A beautiful sunset, not the end of a hard day's work, was the guise for unwinding. When you start unwinding the already unwound citizens of the Keys, you don't have much slack to work with. The thought of having to go to work the next morning acts as a time restraint for many cocktail hours on the mainland. This restraint was lacking in a community that had sought to

126

isolate itself from the workaday world. Limiting cocktails to an hour was pretty much out of the question.

Donnie soon tired of these inevitably boring social gatherings. Cocktail hours seemed to hold otherwise interesting people at a distance during noisy, fragmented, often interrupted conversations. He certainly had never needed an excuse to drink or to talk. His preference was small, dinner parties. These provided a forum for more meaningful dialogue, and the food was usually healthier.

Don had pretty much outdistanced his past, at least the part that he was racing against, when fate entered into the picture. It was a year after his arrival on Big Pine when one of his, now not so new, neighbors discreetly approached him with a proposition. How would Don like to make some big bucks? Don listened as Jimmy, a neighbor from across the street, explained how a guy who had a boat about the size of Donnie's Robalo and who possessed the requisite boating skills, might qualify for a high-paying job. He was a little hesitant, but Don asked Jimmy to continue. The job entailed making a little run off the coast of Cuba, rendezvousing with a small freighter, loading some coke, and delivering the cargo to Jimmy's dock. There would be two other boats involved. If he accepted, Don would receive a one-third advance, followed by one-third at delivery, and the final payment after Jimmy sold the cocaine. Don was surprised that Jimmy had approached him, since they did not know each other that well.

What trait did Don exhibit that attracted these guys to him? His free-spirited lifestyle was being compromised by the need to fund it. His youthful scorn of creature comforts had mellowed, but he could hardly be accused of living a life of luxury. Donnie had asked Jimmy for a little time to think it over. There were still a few coffee cans buried in Mom's backyard, but he was spending money faster than he had anticipated. He no longer used cocaine, and he wasn't sure that making it available to others was a good idea, but if Don didn't, someone would. Situational morality versus economic necessity, another battle was resolved in favor of taking care of number one. Still, there was something about Jimmy that didn't sit well with Don, but at least he would not be dealing directly with the Colombians.

The scenario was the same. The Gulf Stream had to be crossed. This time the Stream was flowing in a more easterly direction and the distances were somewhat longer. It was a trip across open waters of about eighty-five miles. The freighter was actually inside Cuban waters, and Don was surprised when Jimmy told him that there was nothing to worry about from the Cuban authorities. As far as Don was concerned, Jimmy had not paid enough attention to the details. A bright moon made for a pretty crossing. Unfortunately, it also made for a bold and conspicuous silhouette of the Robalo as it approached the Keys, a silhouette which would also be visible on the radar screens of the DEA. Convenient that the balloon, which suspended the antenna used to detect surface contacts was down for repair that night. Maybe Jimmy's planning had not been that bad.

It was a smooth trip. Jimmy told Don that when he dropped his cargo, he would have the second installment of his fee about a week after. This annoyed Don. That would make the payment seven days past due, and Don had always had a low tolerance for late payments. He paid his bills on time, usually in cash, and he expected others to do the same. The money was destined for his underground safe deposit box, so it was not like the delayed payment was a major inconvenience; however, there was a principle involved.

Ten days later, Jimmy gave Don half of the second payment that was due, and he promised that the other half would be paid in a few more days. Don asked about the final third, since, in theory, it was also due now. Jimmy had told him that he was experiencing some problems, but Don didn't need to worry.

When Don got the balance of the money due him, he would be in pretty good shape, financially. He did worry a little about his brother's law of "Recurring Non-Recurring Events." Ralph had told him that, while working with financial statements and forecasts, he had become aware of phenomena that he described as "Recurring Non-Recurring Events." This law applied to life as well as financial statements, according to his brother. The law implied that unanticipated events occurred on a regular basis, so they should be anticipated. The events themselves might be different, but what you could rely on was the fact that an unanticipated event would occur. Perhaps this was Murphy's Law at work, but Don had tested it, and Ralph's law sure held true in his life. Expect the unexpected. Still, Donnie felt he would be in good enough financial shape to absorb some zingers, should they come his way, which he was sure they would.

Don still enjoyed his volleyball; however, the only consistent place that he could find a game was the beach at Key West. This presented a couple of problems. First, it was a fifty-two mile round-trip drive in his old Bronco. Second, the trip back to Big Pine had to be taken at slow speed when under the influence. The reason being was that after a hot day of beach volleyball, a few drinks by these highly tuned athletes usually led to a few more. When Don could not find shelter for the evening with either a fellow player or an adoring fan (there were fewer of these as he got older), he would undertake the drive back to Big Pine Key. There were twenty-six miles of darkened road that had to be traversed. Twenty-one bridges stood between him and the security of his pillow. Passing through such colorful keys as Torch, Ramrod, Cudjoe, Boca Chica, and Big Coppitt, he often wondered how these small islands had derived their names.

The drive was just long enough for him to listen to his eight-track tape of Hank Williams. He did have one other old tape of the Moody Blues, but he found little solace in that tape during these evening quests to find Big Pine.

This bold smuggler had successfully evaded authorities every time that he had come across the Gulf Stream, but he rarely evaded them slowly winding his way up U.S. 1. There was only one road available and the cops knew it. If his driving was erratic, they pulled him over. Don was not a dignitary, nor was he a tourist. He was a character, and

129

that was good enough to get him preferential treatment, either a call for a cab or a ride in the patrol car back to his house. It was a pain to fetch his Bronco the next day, but one thing he could be sure of was that it would be there. Who would steal what appeared to be a ditched vehicle waiting for the grim wrecker?

A couple of over-zealous rookies had actually given him tickets. Don understood, and did not hold it against them. They would learn. Mothers Against Drunk Driving, had they been a factor during this era, might not have been so forgiving, but at the hour that Don plied the road, all kiddies should have been tucked safely in their beds. Actually, Don didn't like to be out on the road at that hour because of the danger posed by a drunken tourist, who had just drowned his sorrows to the point of being one drink away from unconsciousness, driving an unfamiliar tank; or a fisherman driving a patched together large old V-8 powered piece of metal. At least the fishermen knew the roads.

At the end of his first year on Big Pine, Don renewed his lease. Again, he paid his rent for the full year in cash. Old friends began to catch up with him. It was not like he left a forwarding address when exiting the Bahamas. Word of mouth was the only means of tracking him down. Donnie had not moved to the Keys to escape his buddies. It was the fringe element that held no interest for him.

To a man, his pals were surprised at what they found when they visited Donnie. The biggest shock was Phil Donahue. On weekdays, Donnie did not begin his outdoor activities until after watching the Phil Donahue show. This was a shock. Most of his friends could not remember Donnie ever watching anything but a sporting event on TV. He didn't even accept phone calls during the show. Wow! What was happening here?

When Phil signed off, Don signed on. He would suddenly become his old self—ready to go diving or fishing, play volleyball, and ready to party. No drugs, though, and his buddies were impressed.

Many of his friends had kids now, and they were welcome at Donnie's as long as they conducted themselves properly. Donnie loved to take kids diving, exposing them to the beauty of his favorite habitat. The inevitable reaction of the kids brought him much inner satisfaction, and he had a great rapport with them. He missed the kids in the Bahamas, so when any youngster showed up at his doorstep there on Big Pine, that "kiddo" would be in for a treat. Teenaged boys, in particular, seemed to hold Donnie in awe. He was so different. A little gruff, a little demanding, but he treated them like men. It was like a mini outward-bound experience, but it was a lot more fun. Donnie's buddies, who were dads, really appreciated the way he responded to their kids. He treated daughters about the same as he treated sons. Some enjoyed it; others did not, but none ever forgot a visit with Donnie.

A broken romance inflicted a grievous wound on Don during that second year at Big Pine Key. His on again off again affair with Tonia imploded. The violence that accompanies an implosion may have been missing, but the damage was not. Donnie's ego suffered what may have, ultimately, been a mortal blow. Donnie had finally bitten the bullet and asked Tonia to marry him. Unfortunately, the bullet ricocheted back in his face. Tonia had evolved over the years, just as Don had. The problem was that she was moving in a different direction. She had her nursing career, and in Donnie's absence, Tonia had found another guy.

Maybe he overreacted when he lost control on that day a few years ago. Don had been upset at Tonia, but even now, he couldn't remember what possessed him to throw all of her belongings from the patio of her second floor apartment into the pool. Donnie had, subsequently, made amends, but he was old enough to realize that women tend to be a little slower in letting go of grudges.

The contemplation of marriage had been a major concession to Don's lifestyle. Although it was not easy, he could understand where Tonia was coming from. What bothered him, when the smoke cleared, was why had he asked in the first place? It sounded to Don like maybe he was getting old. The signs were there. Had he just been ignoring them? He equated aging with diminished capacity and moderation. Neither of these traits would find sanctuary in his inner being.

131

With the help of his trusty vodka, Donnie got on with his life. Fermented potatoes were often used to distill vodka. Several years of poor potato crops had caused the famine in Ireland, and in the end, healthy potato crops had rescued the Irish. So, in their fermented form, they could usher this jilted, hybrid Irishman over the hump.

To help placate his sorrow and to infuse new spirit into his life, Don took a trip to Grand Cayman. His lease was expiring, so what better time to explore new beaches and new reefs? The diving was great, but it seemed everyone else knew this. Don preferred a little more privacy; besides, Grand Cayman was expensive.

Donnie did meet a nice divorcee from Boca Raton. She was visiting the Keys with her daughter. She liked volleyball, and they had met on the beach one day after a hot and sweaty match. Danielle was attracted to this energetic guy with a graying beard. His receding hairline was offset by the length of his mane. He was obviously well liked by the crowd that hung out on that part of the beach. She coyly positioned herself for an encounter. This strategy was not necessary, as Donnie already had his eye on her. Key West was not Boca Raton. They played the dating game under different rules in the Keys. Don was not exactly festooned in finery. The only thing hanging on his body was an aging Speedo, and Danielle had already noted what it seemed to be hanging on. Their initial conversation did not touch on jobs, money, or signs of the zodiac. There was touching though. It was harmless when Don put his hand on Danielle's shoulder, but it established a bridge for exchanging life forces, and the bridge was soon crowded with traffic. Feelings and energy were crossing this invisible span with great intensity. They both decided that it might be a good idea to sit down, talk, and have a drink.

Don invited Danielle back to Big Pine Key and she accepted. Her daughter was a little too old to send for a milkshake, so Don introduced her to the son of one of his neighbors. The kids hit it off. Privacy was now assured. Danielle and Donnie did not need to re-establish any bridges. Their bodies had closed all the gaps between them as they writhed, locked

132

in a passionate embrace. Danielle thought, not bad for a guy who could cook too. It was the beginning of a short, but torrid romance.

Ultimately, they shared several memorable weekends together, but the relationship was doomed to fail. Geography and differing lifestyles were the cause of its demise.

Don began spending more time than ever in Key West. After two years, the sheriff's deputies were getting a little fed up with his late-night erratic commute. It was time to hitch up the wagon and head west, old man.

⌒ CHAPTER TWELVE ⌒

"The Strangler Fig is a slow growing vine.
Starting high in the tree,
Its trip to the ground is often sublime.
But the death of the host is preordained;
Choked by the grip of this natural baggage,
Relentless, relentless it cannot be restrained."

AUTHOR

THE TRIP WEST TO STOCK ISLAND, a bedroom community on the eastern edge of Key West, was all of twenty miles. Most of the bedrooms were situated in trailers, which made up the preponderance of the homesteads on this islet. Tucked away, only a couple of blocks from busy U.S. Hwy. 1, was a sprawling, not-so-mobile home community. If noticed at all by the tourists heading into Key West proper, it was usually equated to the other side of the tracks in their hometowns. It was populated mainly by two distinct classes with a smattering of eccentrics rounding out the demographics. The first class was so lacking in class that classifying them was impossible. They are young, and lived on Stock Island because it was the only place they could afford. Fishing and living off of the tourists provided little hope for attaining the American dream. They quickly realized that dreams were elusive, and dreams don't pay the rent. When they got a respite from work, those young adults drank hard and made babies. When there was no work, they drank hard and made babies. A few lucky ones escaped to the mainland, but it was tough to leave the Keys. Initiative and incentive melted away under the scorching, brilliant sunsets and the tequila sunsets consumed in dark, little trailers.

The second primary class was comprised of older souls, who had drifted in from all across the nation. Newton may have redefined his laws on gravity if he had known about Key West. The pull that it exerts on wandering folks is not easily explained. Just looking at a map of the USA, Key West appears enticing. It must be impervious to cold weather, marital problems, job problems, and problems in general. White collar workers, disgusted with inept bosses and corporate hierarchies; blue collar workers, tired of punching in and punching it out; ex-servicemen, tired of a life of discipline; and countless others gravitated slowly but inexorably south and then west toward this end of the line.

The eccentrics were drawn for varying reasons, and when added to the mix of mainstream Key West, you had a community not replicated anywhere else in the world.

As the sun rises, the city would come to life slowly, not unlike New Orleans. Later in the day, swarms of tourists, walking on Duval Street or riding on sightseeing trams, made Key West hard to distinguish from any other tourist oriented community. Some might have tagged it as a smaller version of Charleston. With the approach of evening, the leopard would change its spots once again. Key West would surge to life, now reminding one of a warmer, flatter version of San Francisco.

The locals would sleep in and pace themselves through the heat of the day. The tourists would come looking for a party. Key West was a certifiable, bona fide catalyst. It would be no accident when the bars would swing into full gear, and the town would come alive. An occasional thunderstorm would clear the streets and swell the watering holes to capacity.

Would this kind of atmosphere appeal to Donnie? Hell, only minor modifications of lifestyle were required. He fit right in. Lying low in his air conditioned trailer; watching *Donahue*; emerging for a game of volleyball; diving on a favorite reef; taking up a position on a barstool; wooing the visiting senoritas—Don was in his element. The Conch Republic became his new domain.

Don had rented a trailer on Stock Island. It was located in the upscale part of the sprawling mobile home community. Situated at the end of a little finger canal, he was able to access a main channel that led to the ocean. A small backyard made loading and unloading his boat an easy task. First time visitors, who wound their way through the maze of trailers, could not help but wonder—is Don losing it?

Preconceived notions were soon shattered. Sitting and talking with Don, looking around, you soon realized that this new home was a natural evolution in his free spirited lifestyle. The house was not big, but it was big enough for a guy who spent so much time outdoors. It had two bedrooms, a kitchen, and a Florida room added to the side. There was a dishwasher, a microwave, and a TV. His boat was parked in the water behind his house, and his Bronco was parked out front. Situated only minutes away were ocean reefs, ocean beaches, sandbars, and bar bars. And guess what? It was cheap and he did not have to worry about maintenance or mowing the yard. There was no condo association either.

This was not keeping up with the Jones's; it was setting the standard of simplicity (a standard that most people seem to overlook in their quest to accumulate). Reading *Walden Pond* had influenced Don's entire life. There had been moments of excess, but these were usually artificially induced by cocaine and alcohol.

The bane in his life continued to be alcohol. It exerted its influence daily. Don realized that he had a drinking problem. Actually, he had known this for quite a few years. He had vivid memories of his encounters with shrinks while at the Naval Academy. Those encounters, combined with his independent nature, precluded him from seeking counseling for alcohol dependency. Don felt that the only one who could help him with his drinking problem was he, himself, but his self was just not up to the task.

There was a vexing problem wearing on Don. He had not received his third payment from Jimmy. Several trips back to Big Pine had

Don With Cuda Behind His Stock Island Abode

produced only empty promises. Jimmy was not a nice guy, so Don had been using diplomacy in his efforts to collect what was due him. In fact, Jimmy had a reputation for violence, although Don had never personally witnessed the darker side of this importer. Don had calculated this money into his living standard, and while it was not a major issue yet, it could be.

Don, due to his eccentric behavior, had not been embraced by the Conchs. The Conchs were the real locals of Key West or "Cayo Hueso" (Bone Key), as the Spanish named it. The bones were those of the Indians, who had died there from diseases introduced by the early explorers of Key West. You had to trace your roots back through at least three generations to attain Conch status. The more recently arrived locals, though, readily accepted Don into their ranks.

HE HAD A BRIEF AFFAIR WITH PAM, a married lady, who worked as a waitress at a little dockside cafe. Her husband was a sailor at the Boca Chica Naval Air Station, and he was gone a lot. Don did not usually involve himself with married women for more than a night. He figured that married women were entitled to a one-night fling, since their husbands probably did the same thing. But anything longer than that brought complications, and even in his mid-forties, he was trying to keep things simple.

One night, while carousing the town with his friend Dave, Donnie had an encounter, not with a UFO, but with a grounded, personable lady who tended bar at PT's, a little tavern on Caroline Street. Dave did the introductions, and soon Sandy and Donnie were locked in conversation. The thrice-divorced Sandy felt an attraction to this guy who had been a stranger less than an hour before. When Sandy told Don that she was trying to get a recently purchased dive shop off the ground, he was excited. Sandy and

138

Don ran into each other a few times around town. One afternoon, Donnie invited Sandy to join him and some friends for a cookout at his place on Stock Island. She accepted and a good time was had by all.

It was not Don's love of diving that led him to the dive shop at the base of the pier in Key West. Adorned in one of his dress Speedos, he showed up with a bouquet of flowers for the struggling new owner. Sandy was older than Don, but he was attracted to this independent lady who had built up a nice little business. She had worked hard to get where she was.

The next few days Donnie found himself stopping by the dive shop on one pretense or another. Bantering with Sandy was his primary reason for visiting. With the help of her son and son-in-law, she had the business heading in the right direction. Sandy turned out to be intelligent, as well as hardworking. The little light that went on when Don felt a heightened attraction was illuminated. An old saying came into his head: "It is better to light one little candle than to curse the darkness." Sure, Sandy was older, but he enjoyed her company, and that dark, aging trailer could sure use some light. Don had decided on a strategy for recruiting a new roommate. One evening, Donnie just happened to show up around closing. Perhaps Sandy would be interested in joining him for a drink? She was. Cocktails led to dinner, dinner led to dessert, and dessert was served back at Donnie's metal bungalow. For both, the relationship may have lacked the passion and fervor of earlier years, but it possessed other qualities. It was softer and more natural. It was comfortable and satisfying. There were moments of intensity, but they did not come at the cost of throwing the last log on the fire.

Sandy began spending more and more time with her young lover. Well, Donnie was a few years her junior. The relationship was working for Don. On the pretense of good economics, they mutually decided that cohabitation might be a good idea. Besides his marriage to Rachel, his proposal to Tonia was the only time that Don had considered a permanent roommate. Pretty Patty had been a constant companion, as had been a couple of others, but Donnie had no room to share, at the time.

Was he giving up his freedom, or was he freeing himself of the burden of the constant search for sexual fulfillment?

Don looked in the mirror. He saw the same thing that any in his generation would see. The face staring him in the eyes was wearing glasses perched below solid rows of wrinkles and a forehead that had expanded. What was left of his hair was tinged in gray. His beard masked the sagging skin of the lower jaw, but he knew it was there. The eyes still sparkled but a few lumens less than at their peak capacity. Leaving the bathroom mirror, Donnie headed for his easy chair. Sitting, he pondered the words of John Donne in *Devotions upon Emergent Occasions*: "No man is an iland, intire of it selfe." Yeah, maybe this arrangement with Sandy was a natural evolution.

Shortly after Don moved to Stock Island, his nephew, Scott, paid him a visit. The little blonde haired kid, who had been mesmerized by Pretty Patty some eleven years earlier, had grown up. Scott had graduated from high school, and was waiting for his eighteenth birthday, when he would be heading to marine boot camp. Scott was a certified diver, and Donnie truly enjoyed hosting his own kin. He took Scott with him on his daily rounds of the reefs, to the beach volleyball court, and to his local watering holes. He remembered his own uncles taking him and Ralph on their rounds many years ago in Boston.

While Scott was visiting, Don noticed a couple of burns on his arm. He inquired as to their origin. Scott told him that in an effort to impress a girl that he cared for, he had held his arm over the open flame of a lighter as long as he could until she had told him to stop. Don, shaking his head, said he had never met a girl that he wanted to impress that badly. Scott calmly looked him in the eye and replied, "That's too bad."

Scott headed back home before leaving for his stint in the marines. Don enjoyed the visit. Scott handled his uncle's gruff and demanding behavior very well. He shouldn't have much trouble with the marines, Don thought. Donnie invited him back after the marines had toughened him up, but he knew that this was already one tough kid.

140

FOR SOME REASON, his location in the Keys seemed a great distance from his hometown of West Palm Beach. The Abacos, with all of their serenity, were closer to West Palm or North Palm Beach, where his mother now lived, than was Key West. Trips north were infrequent.

He did, however, have to make occasional trips to his old neighborhood bank. On one of these trips, Don got it in his mind that there had been a bank error. Most people reconcile their bank accounts every month or two, and while some people are not satisfied unless they reconcile to the penny, others are content to just be close. Not Don, he had a vague idea over the years how many coffee cans were buried in his mom's backyard, and now he thought one can might be missing.

A thorough reconciliation would require re-landscaping her backyard. At ten thousand dollars a can, a one-can error was significant. In the end, Don felt that tearing up his mother's yard would only serve to fluster her.

In recent years, his mother had incurred his wrath for what, in retrospect, were silly little reasons. Being out of some key food item, having no ice, or forgetting where something was and not being able to put her hands on an item fast enough would trigger verbal abuse. These blowups were directly related to his heavy cocaine period and/or an excess intake of alcohol. His mother suffered from high blood pressure and those incidents added several points to her readings.

The incidents were history now. Don regretted them. His mother had sacrificed so much for him and his brother when they were growing up. Small in stature, she had been large in life. His mother had been a balancing force to a dad who, although good-natured, drank and gambled and tended to be irresponsible.

Everyone who met his mother liked her. Alice was such a kind person. All of Don's lady friends over the years had loved her, and most still dropped by from time to time.

When Don was growing up, she did not drive. With his dad away a lot, this created logistical problems. On shopping days, the two brothers would meet her at the supermarket, and they would carry the groceries the several

141

blocks back to the house. There was no washing machine, so the laundry had to be lugged two blocks to the Laundromat. There was no dishwasher, so Don and Ralph shared that chore. Don recalled that the three of them had made a pretty good team.

After his dad died, he and Ralph encouraged her to get her license. She only drove for about four years before a fender bender shattered her confidence. During the time that she had her license, she still preferred to walk. She only put about six thousand miles on her little Chevette in four years. The Chevette was a present from Don. He had splurged during that period when he was burying coffee cans.

Hugging was not big in Don's family; if it had been, Donnie would have given his mother lots of bear hugs. Instead, she had to settle for less obvious signs of affection. An arm around the shoulder conveyed more than one might imagine.

Don sensed that his mother was slipping a little. She was slow to recognize his voice when he called. Her speech was a little more hesitant. She was in her eighties, and she still lived alone and managed her little house. She was independent. Don recognized that trait, so he was slow to advise her that a change might be necessary. In any case, he felt ill suited to deal with her problems of aging. Ralph was going to have to deal with that. Don knew that his brother had his own problems, but he felt confident that Ralph would handle it.

WITH A NEW ROOMMATE, Donnie's life began to fall into a routine. A typical day would start with a bowl of cereal and a glass of orange juice. He would add a little sugar on the cereal and a little vodka in the orange juice. Next, he would read the paper and watch *Donahue*. Then, weather permitting, he would crank up the boat, stop at the fuel dock for ice and gas, and head for his targeted reef for the day. Frequently, he would stop and pick up Ernie on the way.

Don had obtained a commercial license, which allowed him to sell fish and lobster to the local fish houses. This was done on a cash basis. The money earned supplemented his diminishing stash contained in soil-deposited coffee cans. He was taking his diving a little more seriously these days. With his diving buddy, Ernie, who was a Key West firefighter, he would scour the reefs. The two were a good team. Ernie was his best partner since Kevin those many years ago in the Bahamas. Ernie's regular job called for him to work a twenty-four-hour shift, and then he had the next two days off. The diving provided him with supplemental income. Risking your life or serious injury as a firefighter was a labor of love, not one that was going to make you a rich man. Weather and schedules permitting, they would get underway after the sun was high enough to light the reefs, but before it influenced the afternoon sea breezes.

By the time you factored in the cost of fuel and the cost of boat repairs, they did not clear much; but both loved just being out there. This was the true meaning of positive cash flow.

With a boatload of lobster tails or fish, they were off to the local wholesalers. A short nap, and by early afternoon Don showered and changed his Speedo. A ten-minute Bronco ride and he was at the Smather's Beach volleyball courts. Sipping his afternoon drink of Yoo-hoo! and vodka, he would converse with the locals before starting a game. Two hours later, after showering off the sand and sweat, and with the approach of evening, it was back on the Bronco for the trip home to the barn (no trips to the bars, as in the old days).

He and Sandy would have dinner and then settle in for an evening of reading. Sleep would catch up with him in the same manner as it had his dad (no ashtray full of ashes or no stale beer, but a half finished Yoo-hoo! with the vodka rising to the top).

There were breaks in the routine, lest you worry that Don had fallen into a total rut. One day, he received an SOS phone call from his friend, Dave. Dave was in distress. He was not in mortal danger; he was just a mortal with a common problem. His new and untried girlfriend had mutinied and left him crewless in Nassau where Dave had sailed from Key West. He had another charter scheduled. Could Don lend him a hand? The next morning Don arrived at the airport in Nassau.

143

Their departure from Nassau was interrupted when a large tanker spilled asphalt into the harbor. The tanker's insurance company asked all boats that had suffered damage as a result of the accident to remain in port while they assessed the losses.

If you were going to be delayed, Nassau made a nice place to be stranded, especially if you were anchored just off of Paradise Island. Each evening, Don would venture into the casino, not to seek his fortune, but to be entertained and to entertain. His wry remarks delighted both the dealers and the other players at the five-dollar tables. Dave's job was to round up a couple of ladies for the later night's activities. Loneliness did not plague them at their anchorage. Had the boat been a floating bed and breakfast resort, the no vacancy sign would have been posted every night.

One day, while shopping for grub in downtown Nassau, Don ran into an old volleyball-playing friend, Ray. Ray was a boater as well as a volleyballer. A common denominator possessed by many of Don's friends was a love of the water and a passion for volleyball. Ray was on his way back to the States, but he could delay his trip long enough for a couple of afternoons of diving in the sand in pursuit of saving a point or two.

Most men of Don's age were chasing golf balls around a manicured course in their electric golf carts after paying a fee for the privilege. Don preferred the exertion of volleyball. Maybe it was easier for a guy with failing eyesight to see. In any case, a couple of hours of volleyball provided plenty of exercise and a true aerobic benefit. Don didn't need to join a health club as many of his contemporaries did. The game also allowed him to network with his friends. Deals of a different sort were often concluded at these beach side country clubs.

Finally, after about ten days, they got underway for Georgetown, which was located on the southern tip of the Exumas.

After five days, Dave and Don tired of diving. They dove each day as they proceeded south, but since they were both such proficient divers, it would only take a short time to come up with dinner. Neither had a desire to spear any excess fish or lobster. It was not a sport with them. They had nothing to prove to each other.

As they approached the anchorage at Warderick Wells, the discussion turned to women. Both complained about the lack of female companionship available in this remote stretch of the Exumas. Dave told Don to think positive. Maybe they would run into four horny nurses from Chicago. It was just a lighthearted remark.

They anchored in the narrow anchorage at Warderick, and decided to take their dinghy on a scouting run up through the cluster of about a half-dozen boats that had beaten them there. It was a small anchorage, and they were soon off of the stern of a trimaran with two attractive ladies sitting topside. Dave's boat, the *Commander*, was also a trimaran, but on that day it was an icebreaker too.

With the first encounter barriers broken down, there was an instant bonding. The guys liked to think that this instant rapport was the result of the girls being attracted to their physiques, not the similarities in their boats, but the important thing was that they had struck pay dirt.

Don and Dave invited the girls for dinner on Dave's boat, and the girls reciprocated by inviting the guys for cocktails. The four of them got along famously. Two couples, two boats, two sources of privacy, even numbers sure made it easy. Dave and one of the girls returned to the *Commander* for a sleepover. Donnie remained as a hostage on the girls' trimaran. It was the kind of evening where desires for "sweet dreams, pleasant dreams" were dispensed with prior to going to sleep. As a testament to positive thinking, it should be noted that both girls were nurses, although they were not from Chicago.

The *Love Boat*, as the guys had dubbed the gals' trimaran, would be stopping in Georgetown. When they arrived in Georgetown, Don and Dave spent one more evening with their newfound friends. The girls then departed on their boat for Jamaica to pick up a cargo. Dave and Don were left to take on all challengers at the local volleyball court. Playing as many as six opponents at a time, they fared well. Those countless afternoons at the beach volleyball courts in Key West paid off.

Don helped Dave with his charter, which took place in the waters surrounding Georgetown.

After thirty days with Dave, it was time for Donnie to get back to his routine in the Keys. Three connections and a few hours later, Don was unloading his Igloo luggage at his trailer on Stock Island.

THE FACT THAT DONNIE asked Sandy to marry him was a strong indicator of his comfort level. She graciously declined. A fourth husband would indicate that she had not learned too much from the past. Don took her rejection in stride. This could be construed as an indication that the old warrior was mellowing. Not so, a sudden loss of temper would quickly squelch that illusion.

Don kept a tidy trailer. He stopped short of being anal-retentive, but he liked to know where everything was. Sandy was an organized person too. This minimized confrontations, which invariably resulted when an item became misplaced. Don's anger would surface if he had to search too long for a missing item. Where had Sandy put it? She knew better than to confront Don. It was, of course, her fault. Sandy would quietly locate the object of his wrath. It was not worth it to prove that Don might have forgotten that he had misplaced the item. With peace restored, she could get back to her crossword puzzle.

Strange, the path less chosen seemed to converge with all other trails.

⌒ CHAPTER THIRTEEN ⌒

As I've no idea of the time,
No inkling of the place
Where I shall seek that Blest Abode,
To find a vaster space—
To friends I've known on sea or land,
Who wonder when or how—
Rather than wait until too late,
I'm saying "Goodbye" now.

"GOODBYE," BY C. H. LIGHTBOURN

THINGS HAD BEGUN TO UNRAVEL FOR DON. As he sat on the cooler, which also served as the seat on his seventeen-foot runabout, he reflected on the last year. It was 12 April 1993, and Don was forty-nine years old. He was trying to regain his composure. Only an hour earlier, he had blown a hole in his trailer with a .25 caliber pistol.

Sandy and he had argued over an incident that had occurred several months earlier. Someone had slipped something into one of his drinks, and that had precipitated some bizarre behavior on his part. Although Don had more than dabbled in marijuana, cocaine, and alcohol, he always made the choice. He basically knew where those substances were going to take him. The high that he experienced from what must have been LSD took him by surprise. Don did not like those kinds of surprises, especially when

147

Last Picture of Don With Nephew Scott Several Months Before Don Disappeared

they led to embarrassing behavior on his part. What upset Don was that Sandy had known who had spiked his drink. She had not said anything for fear of how Don might react towards the perpetrator.

A concerned neighbor had heard what sounded like a shot, and when he came to inquire, he found Don loading his boat. He asked if everything was okay. Don apologized and said that he had shot into the trailer "for effect." He wondered if the neighbor had noticed how confused and upset he was. In a trance, he loaded some gear onto his boat.

THE RUNABOUT ROCKED GENTLY on the light chop of the Atlantic. Don had anchored the boat about five miles out near the Western Sambo Reef. The weather in south Florida from mid-April to mid-May was often marked by calm breezes and sunny, mild days. Most of the tourists had retreated north, and the summer vacationers were still hard at work. Light winds made for ideal diving conditions, but on this particular evening, Don's thoughts were elsewhere. He had destroyed the serenity of the evening, and now, three hours later, he was trying to recapture it. What had caused him to go off the deep end over such a trivial matter?

This matter may have been trivial, but there were other problems in paradise. At this point in the narrative of Don's life, it might be helpful to consider some recent events.

Fifteen months earlier Don had retired his Robalo. Don's boat finally succumbed to the cumulative pounding of the sea. Gas fumes were the first indication that a fuel tank had ruptured. When the boat was pulled for repairs, the owner of the boatyard said that it sure felt heavy. He and Don decided to weigh it. Turned out that some hairline cracks had allowed the water to seep into the foam flotation below the deck. The boat was designed to be self-bailing. No water was supposed to reach this part of the boat, so there was no real way to remove it. No wonder the boat had seemed sluggish to Don.

His symbol of independence was no longer seaworthy. He could no longer escape to the one place that always provided him shelter from a society that did not understand him or vice versa, the sea. Financially, he was not in a position to replace the boat. Ralph's law of "recurring non-recurring events" had struck again. Don replaced the Robalo with his current, used runabout. With its forty horsepower Evinrude, it was a major step down from the Robalo.

Six months earlier, in September, Don had told Sandy that he was planning some changes by the end of the year. What would Sandy do if he weren't there, was a question that he posed to her.

Then there was the day, about two months earlier, when Donnie had not returned from a diving trip. Sandy sent out her two sons looking for him. They found him anchored in the vicinity of that same Sambo reef. He was just about out of gas, and he said that he had forgotten his glasses. So he was going to wait for the morning light, when the visibility was better, to head back. He was angry with Sandy for sending out her boys to look for him. Donnie told her that their presence had ruined his plans, and to not ever send them looking for him again.

Another thing that seemed unusual occurred in October. His brother, Ralph, had called and offered Don his twenty-foot open fisherman at a bargain price. He wasn't asking for any money now. Don could pay him at an indefinite point in the future. Don thanked Ralph, but said he was planning some changes at the end of the year, and the boat would not fit into his plans.

149

It would seem doubtful that Don's financial condition was a major factor underlying those changes. How could a guy who had not received a paycheck in over twenty-five years, or who had never accepted a penny of unemployment compensation, now be worried about money? This guy who had made a living on the Gulf Stream was now concerned about his income *stream*? His contacts in the import business had been compromised by his problems collecting the money owed from his previous foray into that line of work.

Also, the state was cracking down on holders of commercial fishing licenses. In order to protect those who truly earned their living from the sea, they had drafted new legislation stating that in order to obtain or renew a license, an individual must be able to prove that over fifty percent of their income was derived from fishing or lobstering. This presented a problem for Don. He had worked on a cash basis. Don did not exist, as far as the federal government was concerned. While living in the Islands, he had never filed an income tax return, and when he moved to the Keys, his sporadic income did not justify filing a return, at least in his mind.

One thing that Don did not need to concern himself with in middle age was a bulging wallet. A billfold crammed with the paperwork of life can be a real nemesis to those who have become a little rotund from the good life. Another bulge in the rear is not what most guys are looking for. Donnie's wallet contained a driver's license, a commercial fishing license, and a picture of his daughter. In terms of trappings, Don had been successful in avoiding the various colored plastic cards that many people fill their wallets with. It is as if people equated success with wallet girth.

Two months earlier, Donnie had borrowed a thousand dollars from Ralph, but he did not seem depressed. He also made two cash withdrawals using his mother's visa card. The total was close to eight hundred dollars, and what was unusual was the fact that he never told his mother about the second withdrawal.

Donnie's health was shrouded in secrecy. He had one large skin cancer that he could not afford to have treated. In addition, his liver had been

150

weakened by hepatitis, and his kidneys were showing the effects of years of drinking. He had become hypoglycemic. He could not go long without food. Sandy had encouraged him to seek medical help, but the combination of a lack of money and a distrust of doctors, which he had inherited from his dad, kept medical help at a distance.

Don was also concerned with the fact that Ralph had just undergone a battle with cancer. Even though Ralph had visited him recently and seemed to be doing all right, it was not lost on him that cancer had ravaged his mother's side of the family. A good friend of his from the Islands was waging his own battle with cancer in Daytona. These things preyed on the mind of someone who had never relished the prospect of growing old. Donnie had told many of his friends, as well as Sandy, on several occasions: "I will never see my fiftieth birthday."

Key West Citizen
April 13, 1993

Small boat found drifting.
No sign of owner.

THAT IS HOW THE NEWS MIGHT HAVE APPEARED, had Donnie's disappearance made the paper, but it did not.

It appears that we will never know what was really on Donnie's mind that night. We are only left with conjecture. Perhaps that is what he intended. Did Donnie orchestrate his final dive or were more sinister forces at play? Did this free diver slip the surly bonds of earth, or is he still wrestling with the problems of mortals?

We do know this: Donnie was a highly complex, very intelligent, insightful individual who hid behind a demeanor of macho bravado and a mask of substance dependency (primarily alcohol). He was fun loving and friendly when not under the influence of the demons unleashed by overindulgence.

When his boat was found drifting and awash several miles from where he had anchored, many questions were left unanswered.

A commercial fishing boat, the *Lucky Two*, found it adrift, a solitary and lonely speck on the sea. The evening before it had throbbed with life. It had been captained by an able, if troubled, seaman. There was no sign of foul play or traces of blood. The boat was undamaged, which would seem to rule out the possibility of a collision at sea. It was highly unlikely that Don had accidentally fallen overboard. Don was fully capable of swimming or staying afloat for an extended period.

The boat was towed back to the Coast Guard base.

A bizarre find the next day did little to clear up the mystery. A diver found a blue duffle bag containing Don's passport, a tee shirt, and the case for his glasses. The duffle bag was attached to one end of his anchor line. This was the end of the line that would normally be attached to the boat. It appeared that the line had been purposely undone in order to

152

secure the duffle bag to it. Either Donnie or someone else was leaving a clue. The anchor itself was imbedded in a reef that would have been a logical spot for him to spend the night (somewhat open, but away from the more protected but mosquito infested mangroves). He had spent an undetermined amount of time anchored on this popular reef in the past. The fact that the anchor with the duffle bag attached was found within forty-eight hours would seem to corroborate this line of reasoning. Did Donnie leave this clue, or was it someone else?

The Coast Guard report indicated that there was a partially consumed cup of coffee still in the drink holder. Closer scrutiny on their part would have revealed a half empty, or half full, if you will, Yoo-hoo! and vodka.

Missing from the boat were his wallet, his .25 caliber gun, his fins, his mask, and a five-gallon gas tank. Not missing and found later in his Bronco were his driver's license and the remains of his dwindling money supply, thirty-seven dollars. The mask and fins could have easily floated out of the partially awash boat. The same fate could have befallen an almost empty gas tank, but it would have had to be detached from the engine.

Before reaching any conclusions as to Donnie's fate, we should consider a couple of other items.

This intrepid soul who had led a life of adventure had trepidations about the future. We will never know the weight that Donnie assigned to his various problems on that final night of contemplation. Donnie was with the one constant in his life, the sea.

From the information available, one could assume four possibilities surrounding his empty seventeen-foot boat.

The first is that Don just chose to leave Sandy, and to start a new life somewhere else. This does not seem likely, since he could have done this without all the theatrics. And besides, he would never have left his drink, his driver's license, or his passport.

A second possibility is that there was an encounter at sea, and he met with foul play. This, too, does not seem likely. There was no sign of a struggle. From all appearances, Don had left his trailer on the spur of the

153

moment. The spontaneity of his departure would reduce the possibility of a chance encounter. Maybe he didn't leave on the spur of the moment? The argument and the actions that ensued could have been staged; however, that would not have been necessary, if he had planned to meet with someone who might have held a grudge. If he were meeting with such a person, he would have been prepared for an altercation. He did have his gun.

The third and fourth scenarios are somewhat intertwined: suicide and the Witness Protection Program. Jimmy still owed Donnie money, and Don had made a recent trip to Big Pine in an effort to collect it. Based on Don's low regard for those who did not pay their debts, it is possible that he could have turned Jimmy in. Don would not have needed his passport and his driver's license if he were under federal protection. Arguments against this are there is no record of any court proceeding in which Don was a witness, and would they have let Don take his gun under the Witness Protection Program? The gun was missing, which leads to the unhappy likelihood that Donnie used it to end his own life. To fulfill the prophecy that he would not make it to age fifty, had Donnie turned it on himself at some point while his boat was drifting? No body was ever found. This argues against a self-inflicted ending; however, it is a big ocean. For the record, the Coast Guard and his friends mounted an extensive search by air over the water that lasted five days.

Family, friends, and readers of this account are free to draw their own conclusions.

Maybe that is what Donnie really had in mind.

In the end, Donnie was a person just like all of us, only he came in the guise of a *free diver* and maybe he was no match for the Black Fairy.

Donnie's old friend from Treasure Cay, C. H. Lightbourn, may have been prophetic when he wrote the following poem several years earlier:

THE SEARCH

My neighbor's a wise and kindly man,
Versed in the ways of the sea,
Knowing the ways of the sudden squalls—
Greatly concerned for me.

"The sea is vast, and the waves rise high;
I know, and my words are true;
If you don't return as you've always done,
Where shall I look for you?"

I thought the matter over,
And then I spoke aloud:
"There's a bit of seaweed floating free,
And overhead a cloud.

Where sea and sky unite as one,
And gulls fly far and free:
Where tuna roam their own domain,
There you may look for me.

Dolphin and 'Cuda know the way—
They'll aid in the search for me;
The cloud I found may still be there,
And the seaweed floating free.

So should you search for me, friend,
Don't look just anywhere:
Remember the cloud, seaweed and gulls,
You're sure to find me there."

155

ABOUT THE AUTHOR

Ralph Leonard was born in Bay City, Texas. He lived in Texas, California, Maine, Colorado, Mississippi, and Louisiana before moving to West Palm Beach, Florida in the mid 1950s.

He graduated from Palm Beach High School, where he was active in sports. After four years in the Navy, where he saw duty on both destroyers and diesel subs, he attended and graduated from Palm Beach Junior College and Florida State University.

He interrupted a career in finance and sold his home in Miami to spend two years cruising on a sailboat with his family.

A bout with cancer led to a reevaluation of his priorities, and after nineteen years with Florida Heat Pump in Fort Lauderdale, he made a decision to move to the mountains of North Carolina where he wrote this story about his brother.

Ralph now resides in Naples, Florida with his wife Eileen.

Any questions or comments?
Contact the author at againstthestream@earthlink.net